ALL THE THINGS
I NEVER TOLD
MY FATHER

ALL THE THINGS I NEVER TOLD MY FATHER

MEMOIR OF A CHILD OF WAR

YONA KUNSTLER NADELMAN

ALL THE THINGS I NEVER TOLD MY FATHER
Memoir of a Child of War

DEDICATION

In memory of my father, Dr. Philip Kunstler, without whom I would not be who I am

In memory of my Uncle Maurycy Spira, without his wisdom I would not be

For my children, Ari and Celina

My grandchildren, Benji, Elan, Maxi, and Jasper

And in memory of all the members of my family who appear in this book but did not survive.

And all those who endangered their lives to help us survive, particularly Pan Professor and his family.

ACKNOWLEDGEMENTS

My most sincere thanks to Ellen Goldin, who helped me in the beginning, and Cassia Korn, Michelle Faulkner, Natasha Grigorov and Pauline Sanchez. Also Heather Brockett for all her reviewing and help in the end.

PROLOGUE

Krakow, July 1945

In the main square called Rynek, the sidewalks are full of people. They have come back to the city from villages and farms, from convents and concentration camps, from cellars, from attics, from bunkers, from holes in the walls.

They come from everywhere, their eyes darting about, searching the passing crowds. They do not talk, or hardly. There is no need for words. Their world is dead. Finished. Everybody here knows that.

When they come upon a friend, some only shake their heads up and down or sideways, while tears fill their eyes and a lump grows in their throats. Then there are those who are searching frantically, obsessively, always hoping. Asking everyone they meet, "Have you by any chance seen or heard about my father, my mother, my sister, my wife?"

I was five years old when the war erupted and twice that age when it ended.

On May 8, 1945, when Germany capitulated, I was told the war was over, but for a long time no one explained that for us the danger had passed.

No one told me who I was or what my real name was, that name I had to forget so completely but which came to me in dreams I could never remember when I awakened.

They told me everyone is dead. There is no family to claim us. As a matter of fact, they said there are no more Jews left in the world. But at that point I didn't care if there were or weren't. I was certainly not one of them. Not anymore. I went to church every Sunday and was even chosen to be a flower girl in a church procession.

And what is a Jew, anyway? By then I didn't know.

I do not remember dates, names, or how old I was when this or that took place. Only seasons. If it happened in winter I remember the snow, or the rainy days of autumn. In spring there were flowers, and in summer the heat and plenty of fruit to eat.

Of those who were part of my life during the war, only two are still alive. The rest are dead.

CHAPTER 1

Leaving Home;
Running Away from Hitler

Something is happening! Something very important, or why would we have come home from summer holidays in such a hurry?

My mother is very upset. Father is preoccupied and irritable. He doesn't want to give me any attention, and he is never that way with me. Something is very wrong. I don't understand why my father sits for hours, glued to the giant Telefunken radio, listening to the strange words coming from all the stations.

I sit and listen with him. "Where is the music?" I want to know. "And all the other programs? What happened to all the children's programs that came out of the radio?" I keep asking my father. What do they mean, those bizarre words, "Coffee in the stratosphere . . . tea in the atmosphere"?

My father won't answer any of my questions; he simply pulls me up onto his lap and, putting a finger to his lips, shows me to be silent.

Thursday night, the thirty-first of August 1939—while we are sleeping, Hitler's army is ready to start World War II by invading Poland.

My father has been called up. He is an officer in the reserves. He has been going on maneuvers for years, maybe preparing for just such a day. Dressed in his uniform, he is ready to go, but first he is told to deliver his wife and daughter to the train station. The women and children of officers are to be evacuated somewhere into the Tatra Mountains, for safety.

Suddenly I am being lifted out of my bed, into my father's arms. He is trying to awaken me slowly. He whispers, "Wake up! Wake up! You have to get dressed; we are leaving."

My Father in Uniform

"Where are we going? It's still night outside." I refuse to wake up.

"We are going to the train station. You and Mama are going back to the mountains." He hands me my clothes and asks me to dress quickly.

There is already a suitcase in the hallway. He calls to my mother and tells her to hurry. She is still in the bedroom, stuffing a small black patent-leather bag with towels, soap, and toothbrushes. From the medicine cabinet she takes bandages, iodine, and a small box with headache powders. She takes out her jewelry from her dressing table drawer, wraps it in a handkerchief, and stuffs it into her brassiere.

"Should we take the inflatable mattress?" she calls to him. "How about blankets?"

"No! No! Take warm coats, sweaters, and comfortable shoes. Only essentials, they said. As little baggage as possible."

We rush to the station. Many women and children stand in small groups. With gas masks in their hands, they listen to instructions given them by a man in uniform who demonstrates how the masks should be worn in case of an attack with gas.

There are many men moving around in the crowd, all soldiers.

My father hands us our masks and we head toward the track where our train is waiting.

Suddenly, a sound I have never heard before—at first just a faint hum, and then a shrill air-raid siren rips through the quiet Friday dawn. Above us, hundreds of little dots pepper the pale blue sky.

Airplanes! It looks like hundreds of airplanes!

In a matter of minutes, bombs explode everywhere.

My Father's commanding officer shouts, "Take cover!" as he and his wife and daughter dive under their automobile. My dad shoves my mother and me under the railroad car as he calls out, "Sir! Not under the auto!"

He hasn't even finished the sentence. A bomb falls. A piece of shrapnel flies through the air and hits the gas tank of the general's car. A giant ball of fire envelops the car and consumes it. When it stops burning nothing is recognizable. There is no car. There are no people.

Friday morning, September 1, 1939—welcome to the war!

Three people died. Right there in front of my eyes! And the war had started only a minute before.

The bombers didn't stay long. They dropped their bombs and left.

Railroad tracks destroyed! Panic and chaos! People running in all directions, not knowing what to do.

As soon as the second all-clear siren is heard, my father grabs my hand and calls my mother to follow. We run out of the station.

In the street, he stops abruptly and looks in both directions. He sees on the other side of the street what he was looking for.

He walks over to the horse and carriage, still standing, waiting for customers as if nothing has happened. As he approaches the driver, the man turns and asks, "Where would you like to go, sir?"

My father doesn't answer but goes forward to where the man is sitting. I'm too far away to hear what they're discussing. They talk and they talk until the man nods in agreement and then climbs down very slowly and hands my father the whip. He counts the money my father gave him, whispers something to the horse, embraces the animal, and kisses his forehead right between the eyes. He tips his hat, bows slightly, and leaves.

My father climbs into the driver's seat and orders us to get in.

My mother looks as if she's in shock. She's totally bewildered, maybe even embarrassed. Finally she asks him, "For heaven's sake, Philip, what are you going to do with this horse and carriage?"

"We are going to leave the city as fast as we can and we are going to the east."

"East? Why east? You don't mean to Russia."

"We will go to Tarnopol. That is not Russia."

"I don't want to go east," she whispers under her breath.

"East is the only way we can go to get away from Hitler."

As we drive through the streets, it's apparent the rest of the city has not been severely bombed, only the train station. The primary target has been the rails.

"That's all they wanted. To paralyze any movements of troops," my father comments, mostly to himself.

It's so early in the morning, and the heat is already horrendous.

From the station we drive directly to my uncle Mooniu's house. Mooniu is my mother's brother. His real name is Mauricy, but we call him Mooniu. His wife, Irena, died four years ago, right after Gaby was born. Gaby is Mooniu's only son, and my favorite cousin. I am exactly a year older than he. We were born one day apart, and ever since I can remember we have celebrated our birthdays together. He is almost like a brother to me. We see each other every day.

Gaby has a governess. Her name is Roza. She talks with my mother every day, sometimes by telephone, sometimes in person. Together they plot his upbringing. Both care deeply about his welfare. Everybody adores Gaby. Dziadziu, my mother's father, is happy that his son has a son who will carry on the family name.

Now Roza opens the door and leads my parents into the sitting room. My mother wants to wash. There is no water, not in the bathroom or in the kitchen. Mooniu wonders what happened. Why is there no water?

"Either the water main has been bombed or they've used up the water to put out the fires." My father seems to know everything.

I want to tell Gaby, who is still asleep, that at the train station this morning I saw the beginning of the war. I hear my father say, "This is what I feared. Now we are at war." Even here at my uncle's house there is a feeling of panic.

What is a war? I don't understand any of it. My father is even more abrupt now than he was before. He sends me out of the room.

Exhausted, I fell asleep.

I must have slept for a long time. While I slept, the whole family has gathered. They are in the other room behind closed doors. Their voices are loud and forceful as they argue.

Dziadziu, my mother's father, is mocking my father's decision to flee as unwise and dangerous. He says, "Let's wait here and see what happens next. You Zionists think you know everything."

As far back as I can remember my father and my grandfather have always been at odds. Dziadziu towers over the rest of the family, not only with his size but also with his powerful personality. He is a true patriarch, with a long white beard, and nobody dares to defy him . . . except my father. My father smokes cigarettes on Saturday, when it is forbidden, is an active and important member of the Zionist party, and generally does as he pleases. Dziadziu doesn't like any of it.

As if he hasn't heard what Dziadziu has said, my father calmly announces, "I'm taking my family and we are leaving. You may do as you please."

Immediately my mother begins to cry. She doesn't know what to do. She is extremely attached to her parents and doesn't want to leave them.

Mooniu pleads with Dziadziu to reconsider. He agrees with my father that we should all leave Krakow as fast as possible.

Frania, Irena's sister, and her husband, Max, have decided to go with us, and at the very last moment, just as we are leaving, Dziadziu changes his mind.

"Gaby, you sit here on my right; you, Yona, on my left." The tone of my father's voice is unmistakably an order. We quickly obey, and he sits down between us. The rest of the family squeezes into the horse-drawn carriage. With the whip in one hand and the reins in the other, he tells the horse to move.

Thus begins our journey east, our flight to safety, away from Hitler. But who is this Hitler, and why is my father so afraid of him, so afraid that we are leaving everything and running away?

CHAPTER 2

Going East

The sun has set. The heat has subsided. It was almost dark when we arrived in a small town called Slomniki. We settled down for the night in an inn owned and operated by a Jewish family. Dziadziu eats only kosher food.

After we ate, my father said to Max and the rest of the family, "Tomorrow we must leave early, even before the sun rises. If the heat wave continues, we will travel in the early morning and late afternoon. Otherwise it will be unbearable."

The next day we are up before dawn. We eat breakfast in silence. Everyone is tired and irritable.

With a familiar gesture, when he finishes eating, Dziadziu cleans his beard, stands up and puts his hands on the table. Addressing my father, this time he speaks softly. "Philip, I've thought it over during the night. We are too old for this journey, so Mama and I have decided to stay here in Slomniki."

Dziadziu (Grandfather) with his beard

Uncle Mooniu made an immediate decision. "You go; take Gaby and Roza with you. I will stay here with Mother and Father."

At this point my own mother becomes hysterical. I have never seen her that way. And it is in that state that she bid good-bye to her adored parents. Sobbing uncontrollably as she's being led to the carriage, she has angry words for my father, accusing him of being the cause of her unbearable pain.

Eventually we are back on the road again. This time Max sits with my father and helps him drive.

During that second day we join thousands of others who, like us, are on the road going east, running away from Hitler. This exodus stretches as far as the eye can see, like a moving rope of strange bedfellows, tied together by the same idea.

There were people on horseback, in cars, and horse-drawn carriages; on bicycles, walking, pulling or pushing carts loaded with their possessions. The pace was so slow that when two enemy airplanes suddenly dove out of the sky spraying bullets, there was no time or place to hide. They flew low, their black swastikas gleaming, and they killed people. They killed men and women and children. Even animals died.

During the attack, my father grabs Gaby and me under his arms and jumps into a ditch. He covers us with his body until the airplanes climb back into the clouds and do not return.

My mother helps some of those who are wounded. She gives away all of her bandages and the iodine she has brought along for us.

9

Death is all around us. We leave behind those who have to bury their dead and continue traveling east, running away from Hitler. Today we are the lucky ones!

From then on we almost never stop moving. Sometimes my father would see a goat or a cow grazing by the road, and we would stop to find the farmer who owned it. We would buy milk, sometimes having to milk the animal ourselves. I learned to drink fresh lukewarm milk and to eat foods I had never eaten before.

Whenever he could, Daddy bought oats for the horse. Otherwise he had to let the animal graze and that took too much time.

We were on the road for days. For the first few days the journey felt like an adventure. Riding on top with my father was fun, and I was not afraid. We ate raw foods that we purchased from farmers. Berries were in abundance because of the time of year, and along with sweet or sour cream, they were daily fare. When we were lucky enough to come across a farm that had just baked bread for the week, we would buy what they were willing to sell. The large round bread, dark and heavy, with the most divine smell, would be devoured in an instant.

Soon the stress of the trip started showing. Sharp words were exchanged between the adults, and the bickering created an unpleasant atmosphere.

Frania is very unhappy. She's constantly cleaning herself with a handkerchief full of cologne, dabbing her underarms and stroking her neck.

My father, irritated by her preoccupation with herself, ridicules her: "Frania, you smell so good that I think you are successfully competing with the flowers!"

"Really, Philip," she snaps, "don't you understand? I am used to having a bath every day. I have been perspiring for days. I am sticky and hot and I smell like these goats! And you won't let me use a drop of your precious water!"

Sometimes it seems there is no war at all, and I forget. Then, there it is again!

We are traveling through open countryside when Frania starts sniffing and sneezing. The air smelled funny. Our eyes start burning and we have difficulty breathing long before the smoke becomes visible.

As the sun set, the dusk seemed thick and dense. Night fell but there was a light in the distance that looked like a reddish setting sun.

At the next turn we came upon the burning forest. There was no way to get through. My father stopped just to the side of the road and went to join a group of people, some of them local farmers stuck with their wagons on the wrong side of this inferno.

It was a small thicket of pines a few hundred yards deep, extending on each side of the road, up and down, as far as the eye could see. It was probably left over from an old forest that has given way to the fields surrounding this little wood.

The pines were very thick and very tall. The fire was burning the tops of the trees where the thin branches and green needles were exploding, making a crackling noise like gunfire.

From afar, it looked like the fire was floating in midair. I never imagined a whole forest could burn.

The farmers were angry. Some of them tried to move through, but their horses reared and absolutely would not go forward.

My father looks into the forest, disappearing into its shadows for a few minutes. When he comes out he tells us he has made up his mind. I am stiff with fear, hardly able to breathe.

Daddy says, "Hela and Frania take all the handkerchiefs and all the towels you have and wet them. Cover your heads and breathe through the handkerchiefs, all of you!"

He climbs up and stands with his feet apart on the front of the rig. The reins gripped tightly in his hands, he commands the horse to move.

The old horse takes off! Weaving through the burning forest, it moves faster than ever before, galloping like a young stallion! In no time at all we are out of the fire, on the road again. All of us in unison shriek with joy, feeling so proud that ours is the only horse willing to brave the danger.

"This calls for champagne!" Daddy says as he hands the water bottle to Max. "Let everyone have a drink!"

By now we look like vagabonds—dirty and unkempt, our clothes rumpled, and our faces covered with soot. As I settle in my mother's lap, she nuzzles her face in my neck, as she often did, with affection. But this time she's repelled by the awful odor of smoke that permeated my hair. "Phooey! You smell awful!"

Frania is looking at my mother and remarks, "I know just how you feel, Hela. Maybe your father was right after all. We should have stayed in the civilized world. For days now, no toilet! No bath!" Frania fumbles with her hanky, looking for a clean spot with which to dab some cologne, the only source of cleanliness left for her. She complains hopelessly that she has never imagined she could survive such deprivation.

Frania is the beautiful older sister of my Aunt Irena, Gaby's mother. She's married to Uncle Max, who is a lawyer, a quiet, sweet man with a bland personality. He loves Frania excessively. Max is probably her senior by quite a few years and indulges her like a child. He cares for her as if she's a hothouse orchid.

I look at Frania with awe. She is always so perfectly groomed. A very beautiful woman, she has dark hair and a porcelain complexion. Her hazelnut eyes are fringed with thick lashes, which she flutters like some actress in a silent movie. Her lips are always perfectly defined with a brilliant red lipstick. She wears her hair in 1930s style: two rolls on each side and a deep wave over one eye. The back of her hair is shoulder-length, flipped under. She has aristocratic hands (my mother says), with blood-red nail polish, only the moons left natural. Magnificent jewelry always adorns her hands and neck. She drapes her body with the most exquisite fabrics. She always looks like she had just stepped out of the pages of a fashion magazine, which my mother loved to peruse. Frania definitely knows the best things in life. I am sure it is no accident that Max is very wealthy and is able to provide her with that style of life. (All of this I did not understand until much, much later.)

Frania is childless—I don't know if by design or fate, which may have been why her figure is still so perfect. She's as slim as a young girl, despite the fact that she constantly gorged herself with chocolates. In Krakow, she had found a store that sold the chocolates wrapped in foil and cellophane, so they stayed intact in her purse. She was never without them. Of course now we are grateful for this fabulous treat. She no longer ate them herself but conscientiously saved them for us children.

Now Frania looks wilted. She calls up to my father, "Listen, Philip, the next farm we come to we must stop! I must clean up and go to a proper toilet!"

"You're dreaming my dear," he calls back to her, "if you think there is a bathroom in any of these farmhouses. Besides, I am not stopping for anything. The Germans are right behind us. We must keep moving!"

With the Germans on our heels, my father will stop now only for relief of the inevitable human needs, and that we do right in the roadside ditch, or in the bushes.

Not all the roads we travel are paved. By now I could distinguish between the clickety-clack of the horse's hooves on the hard asphalt and the softer, duller, tip-tap made while on an unpaved earthen roadway. The even pace at which my father is driving created a steady bounce, very conducive to sleep for a bored and tired child.

I fell asleep; my face nestled in my mother's neck. Slowly, consciousness floated in. I smelled the light, flowery scent of her velvety soft skin. It was still there, underneath all the rest. As I stirred, she moved and tried to change the position she was frozen into when I fell asleep, my body curled on her lap, my arms around her neck. I must have been dead weight for some time because she sighed with relief when I became fully awake. As I tried to sit up, one of my legs would not follow the rest of my body. It was totally asleep, millions of ants slowly crawling under my skin, reminding me that this other leg was still attached to my body.

I was now fully awake and aware of voices in the distant darkness that have roused me from my peaceful sleep. Horses whinnying, water splashing, people shouting and yelling. Dampness fills the night air. We are almost to the riverbank, where a man is coaxing a horse, with a cart, to pull the load out of the river. One man is in the cart, driving. The other is almost invisible, his hands lifted above his head. Only the very tops of his shoulders are sticking out of the water as he pulls the horse. The river is lit sporadically with handheld flashlights.

It was not a very wide river, but its muddy waters seemed to carry the debris floating on top with such speed, past my eyes, that I suspect it had a very strong current. It couldn't have been very deep, for horses were able to walk through with their heads held high, pulling their loads.

Again my father jumped off and went to talk to one of the locals. He hired a tall, broad young man to carry him across the river on his shoulders. As they went across, he measured the depth with a stick he fashioned from a branch off a nearby tree.

Because no one in our group could swim, including my father, he spent some time with the man he had hired, planning the crossing. We were assigned specific places to balance the weight in the carriage. I was sitting on the briefcase that contained towels and toiletries. I was told that the reason I was to sit on the bag was so that I would not get wet, as it placed me high up; it was hoped, above the level of the water.

So much for hope!

The bottom of the river turned out to be unpredictable, and the carriage sank lower than it should have. While my father nervously commanded the horse to go, the tall chap was in the water, walking backwards, pulling the horse with both his hands.

For a split second the horse stumbled, causing the carriage to veer off to the left, sinking deeper into the water. I was now afloat, holding on to the bag beneath me. It took me a few seconds to realize that I was no longer in the carriage. Panic-stricken, I started calling my daddy. There was too much noise and commotion for anyone to hear me immediately. As I floated down the river I screamed and cried for help, and it seemed like years before the young man was swimming over to me and lifting me out of the water to carry me to shore and into the arms of my father.

I was sobbing uncontrollably, trembling from the cold, soaked to the bone, frightened, clinging to my father's neck as I had never done before. With my hands, I was holding the back of his hair so that he could hardly move. Slowly, gently, with his softest voice, he convinced me to let go of his hair. Then, unwrapping my legs from his waist, he seated me on the ground and covered me with something soft and warm, which my mother had put into his extended hand.

It was difficult to hear him talk. My father was speaking . . . but all I could hear was my heart pounding and a voice in my head saying, "You were almost lost." I saw myself floating down the river in the darkness, as the sounds grew more distant and the voices faint, and I knew I would be lost forever.

My mother undressed me, dried me, and warmed me by rubbing my body with a heavy towel. Slipping a dress over my head, she was on her knees as she pressed me to her heart. Holding me that way for a long time, she cried.

Although my father grew impatient as Frania and my mother were wringing the towels and drying the carriage, in a lighthearted tone he said, "Let's get back on the road, Frania . . . now that you've had your bath! You have to forgive me that it wasn't scented, but you have to admit that it was pretty wet!"

"We all know you have a great sense of humor, Philip. Why don't you just climb on top and drive?" she retorted.

Max was studying a map with a flashlight. He climbed on top, next to my dad, and murmured that we should be in Lutsk in a couple of hours.

It was still dark when we reached the outskirts of the city. It seemed deserted. We drove past little houses; most of them had gardens in the front and in the back. There were no lights in any of the windows. For a while my father drove slowly, turning left then right into the little streets. I didn't know what he was looking for, but he later told me that he had a childhood friend living in that town and he was trying to find the street where his friend lived.

As he turned the next corner, he spied something just across the street. There stood a house in which not one window had any glass in it. The dark gaping holes looked weird, opaque. I noticed now that some other houses had glass missing also, and others had shutters that were all closed.

Cautiously, my father approached the house, leaving us all to wait in the carriage. Slowly he moved toward it and then disappeared inside the open doorway. When he emerged, both his arms were beckoning us to come. I ran. This was the first house since Slomniki. I had to see.

My father slowed me down "Be careful! There is glass everywhere!"

One by one, everyone entered the large room. Max explored it with his flashlight. "There is no one here, but it looks like someone had the time to move everything out—lock, stock, and barrel."

"Either that or it was looted," my father suggested.

On the floor, against one of the walls, there was a mound of straw. No other furniture anywhere.

My mother asked, "Is there a kitchen?"

"Yes, there is a kitchen," said Max, motioning with the beam of his light. "Come, I will show you."

She moved behind him into the kitchen. "Oh, look there! Coal! I will be able to make some hot tea! And look at this pot!"

Frania came into the kitchen, and with a dramatic inflection said, "And I have found a bathroom with a great old bathtub. So, I will need the stove and the pot to heat water . . . to bathe my weary body."

My mother found a candle in her travel bag. "Philip, could you light it?"

Daddy reached into his pocket and took out a box of matches. After several attempts it was clear that the matches would not light.

"They are all wet from the river."

"Here, I have another box." Max handed him the box.

There was only one dry match in it.

By candlelight, my mother searched the pantry. It was empty, except in a back corner there was a burlap sack tied with a piece of rope. She untied the rope and exclaimed, "I've found some kasha."

So there it was, kasha cooking on the stove in the middle of the night. Since there were only two spoons, the children ate first. Gaby ate with both hands. He must have been ravenously hungry. Soon he was put to sleep in the corner of the straw pile. The adults were now huddled around the big pot, eating and talking by the candlelight as I drifted off to sleep.

It was wonderful . . . the sound of a guttural belly laugh, happy and explosively infectious. I sat up at once, curious. Who was laughing? What was going on? My mother looked with great affection in the direction of the kitchen. Roza and my father were laughing, she holding her hand in front of her mouth to mute the sound of her giggle. I followed them with my eyes, and there, lo and behold, was Gaby. He was fast asleep, draped over the great big pot, both his arms inside, clutching fistfuls of cold, cooked kasha.

Roza tiptoed over and woke Frania and Max to share with them this moment of pure delight.

My father stopped laughing; abruptly his smile gave way to a frown. "Quiet. I hear something."

We listened to the heavy rumbling sound.

"Everyone get down on the floor and be still," he ordered as he crawled across the room and approached the low, open window from the side. Very cautiously he stood up and flattened his back against the wall, inching his way closer to the opening to catch a peek at the street.

We were low on the ground but we could see now, passing in front of our window, great big olive-green trucks full of soldiers. One after the other they drove down the street as if they were not in a hurry to get anywhere.

My father whispered with surprise, "These are Russians! It's the Red army!"

Stalin and Hitler had a pact for the invasion of Poland. The German army came from the west, the Russians from the east. They met across the River San, swallowing Poland in one big gulp.

My father knew nothing about this at the time. All he knew now was that he wouldn't meet up with Hitler. We were now in Russian-occupied Poland.

The transport stopped and some soldiers leaned out of the back of the truck.

Slowly we got up.

"They seem friendly," Max said to my dad.

Once she felt safe, Frania complained, "If only we had a match, we could heat some water and wash."

My father had an idea. He crouched down to my level, and taking me by the hands, he said, "I am going to teach you two words: SPICHKI and POJZALOSTA, which means, 'Matches, please.' SPICHKI! Now say it with me: SPICHKI."

I repeated it with ease.

He then added, "POJZALOSTA."

Again I repeated the word.

"I will lift you out of the window, to the street, and you go up to one of the trucks, smile, and say, 'SPICHKI POJZALOSTA.'"

I said it over several times.

He lifted me to the windowsill and I swung my feet over, sliding smoothly to the sidewalk.

I am now alone. No other people on the street; only trucks full of soldiers. I walk a few paces to the closest truck. The young Russian soldiers are smiling and calling me over. I don't understand a word they are saying, but I am not afraid. I stand there for a long moment, and then look up at one soldier straight in his eyes, and say, "SPICHKI POJZALOSTA."

Several men put their hands in their pockets and out come dozens of boxes of matches! I run with my loot back to the window.

As soon as I hoist myself onto the windowsill, several pairs of arms pull me back into the room. My quest for fire has been successful. Hallelujah! Frania will finally have a hot bath.

Frania wasted no time. Carefully she rolled up her sleeves, taking a sponge out of her toiletries bag, and soaped it very well. Showing her distaste for work of that sort, she started cleaning the tub. A long while later Frania opened the door to the bathroom and a divine smell of soap and steam filled the air. She came out, her head wrapped turban-like in a towel.

It was well into the morning by the time everyone has had a bath. My father must have thought it was safe to go out because he left and was gone during the time we attended to our toilettes.

Papa came back from reconnoitering. "There are soldiers everywhere, but they seem very friendly," he reported. "I saw people in the streets and I think that by tomorrow everything will be back to normal. I found the telephone number of my friend Dolek Kaczer. When I called him he couldn't believe we were here. Of course we are all invited to their house for lunch."

"Oh, Philip! That's wonderful!" Frania was delighted. "We will sit at a table! With chairs! And eat from plates with forks and knives! How divine! Thank God we are finally back to civilization!"

CHAPTER 3

Aunt Regina and Uncle Motek

Now, for me, the war was over. The Russians had what they wanted and so, it seemed, had the Germans. We were going to join my father's family in Tarnopol. East of the dividing river, the Russians had moved in quickly. In just a few days life was back to normal.

I saw Frania and Max for the last time at the train station. They were taking Gaby and Roza with them to Kolomya, where either Frania or Max had close relatives. I did not realize Gaby and I would be parting. The sadness overwhelmed me, but the moment was lightened when my father told us why no one wanted to buy our horse.

"I must tell you, this was an experience I will never forget," he began. "I went to the square where the farmers come to market and proceeded to offer my horse for sale. One by one the farmers examined the poor animal, smiled, and walked away. When one man asked me how much I wanted, and I told him, he smiled and went away, his eyebrows lifted, looking at me as though I was demented. I ran after him and asked him to make me an offer. Well, at this point he hesitated and said, 'I don't know, maybe he could be a workhorse, and maybe not. Who can tell what a blind animal will do?'"

"Blind?" I said. "Who's blind?"

"Your horse."

"My horse is blind?" I couldn't believe it. Then I thought maybe that was why ours was the only animal willing to enter that burning forest when all the others refused . . . "I guess you never know where your luck will come from!"

When we arrived in Tarnopol there was such a commotion. My uncle Markus's apartment was full of people. Some were relatives, others friends. It was difficult to remember who was who, since I had never seen any of them before.

My father was besieged. From the moment we walked in people hugged him and cried. Everyone wanted to touch him, to shake his hand.

One man, whom I later got to know and love very much, was Oskar, my father's best friend. Oskar did not speak; he cried and held my dad in a tight embrace, slapping him on the back over and over and over. I couldn't understand what was going on until later I found out it was his way of expressing the joy and happiness he felt to see us alive and well and far away from Hitler.

The steady coming and going of people was very strange to me. I had never been exposed to such a crowd of well-wishers.

Both my father's sister, Regina, and his brother, Markus (called Motek), lived in the same building, which belonged to my father's family. My parents and I settled into Uncle Motek's two guest rooms.

Some time in the days that followed, my Uncle Motek suggested that we come to the factory. "After all," he said to my father, "you haven't been here for a long time, Philip. Come and see some of our new equipment." Theirs was the largest candy and chocolate factory in the area, and I couldn't wait to see it. From the stories my father had told me it had to be paradise.

The factory was not far at all. We could see it from Uncle Markus's apartment, just across the square. Hand-in-hand, Daddy and I walked over.

The moment we arrived in this enormous plant I knew everything he had told me was true, only better! The smell was intoxicating, absolutely unbelievable! I could distinguish chocolate, vanilla, raspberries, coconut . . . it was overwhelming!

I didn't know which way to look, or which way to go. I was being dragged by the hand. My mouth must have been hanging open because as my father turned and looked at me he burst out laughing.

"Come on, honey. I want you to meet Mr. Sosnowski. He is the foreman here."

A nice-looking man approached us. He was blond, somewhat portly, and had a jolly face and blue eyes. He wore a white coat and looked like a doctor.

Smiling, he greeted my father. "Hello, Dr. Kunstler. Nice to have you with us."

"Hello, Anthony. This is my daughter, Yona."

"How do you do, Anthony?"

"I am glad to meet you, young lady. Dr. Kunstler, may I show Yona how we make the candy while you go to see Mr. Markus?" He turned to me. "Would you like that?"

"Oh, yes!"

I was already looking at the shiny copper kettle in which a divinely aromatic substance was bubbling. "What is that cooking there?"

"This is sugar for the candy we will be making in this machine." Mr. Sosnowski stationed me to the right of the marble table, where a strapping young man wearing clean white pants and a sleeveless shirt was pouring the boiling sugar into a molding machine. How they did what they did I don't know, but soon the lid of the press fell with a great thump, and magnificent, perfectly shaped raspberries came pouring out of a chute. The ruby-colored sugar was now a hard candy with a soft, raspberry jam center. Mr. Sosnowski reached into the drum and handed me a handful as I looked on in amazement.

Then he led me away to the next area, where a man was doing something so strange that again I could only stare. He pulled and then threw back onto a large hook a thick, shiny mass. The rhythm was absolutely precise. He pulled from the hook on which the sugar was hanging and folded it and pulled and folded until the sugar was pearl-white. Then he took it off the hook and again laid it on a marble slab, from which it was fed to yet another machine that made a hard, white candy with a soft, nutty center.

I was so absorbed by everything I was seeing. I had not realized how hot it was in the factory, where dozens of kettles were boiling, until we entered a room that was much, much cooler. There, at a very large white marble table, sat several women, their hair covered with hairnets. All were wearing white aprons, and their hands were full of chocolate. They looked like children playing in the mud. Each woman had a tray next to her, with some kind of special paper on it, on which she would place the finished chocolates in neatly spaced rows.

One was making chocolate-covered cherries, another made chocolate-covered almonds and walnuts, and yet another was dipping marzipan balls (my favorite)—which by this time I could no longer think of tasting, having sampled all the other sweets made along the way.

My father reappeared, and with a wink at Mr. Sosnowski he asked me, "Well, how do you like it so far? Have you had enough, or do you want to see how they make your favorite ice cream?"

Wide-eyed and very excited, I jumped up and down. "Oh, please, Daddy! Show me how they make ice cream!" I waved good-bye to Mr. Sosnowski and followed my father to another part of the factory.

The ice cream machine looked like an enormous copper kettle sitting inside another even more enormous container, which was filled with crushed ice. Two men poured into the copper kettle, a liquid that smelled like vanilla ice cream and looked like milk.

The man responsible for making the ice cream threw a switch and the inside kettle started spinning—first slowly and then faster and faster. The white liquid sloshed around and through a blade. As the speed increased it began sticking to the side like white paint.

My father touched the inside of the drum with his finger and like magic it was covered with ice cream! He smiled and nodded in my direction. "Go on now; you taste it. When the whole batch is made we will get you the biggest ice cream cone you've ever seen."

Life was not going to be that bad with this factory almost on my doorstep!

For many reasons, living with my father's family now, was very difficult for my mother.

She was accustomed to better things. She had never had to live with anybody, even during the First World War in Vienna. Her family had gone to Vienna with money and they had lived as well there as they had in Krakow. She did not like Tarnopol and did not want to be here. She had no friends. Oskar's wife was much younger, and my mother did not like her. She had little in common with both of my aunts. Undoubtedly she was lonely.

In addition, one of her great problems was that she missed her parents terribly. Not a day went by that she would not reminisce about them. She was now over forty but her attachment to her parents was like that of a small child.

I was not yet of school age, so I was enrolled in a dance academy run by a Russian ballerina, who was in Tarnopol because her husband was a commissar sent to administer the newly conquered land. She spoke Russian to us and was very strict. I don't know how many hours I spent each day in that school, but it must have been several. The rest of my waking hours I spent playing with my cousin Jacob.

Jacob was the only son of my uncle Markus and his wife, Dziunia, a pretty, round-faced woman, somewhat plump and otherwise unremarkable. Jacob, or Kuba, as we called him, was older than I; he was already in school. A beautiful boy, dark-haired with an olive complexion and brilliant blue eyes, he was a very active child, forever thinking up new schemes to get us into mischief. He was definitely the influential male in my life at the time.

One of the games I remember very well was when he tried to entice me under the covers of one of our beds to play the age-old game of "doctor." He told me that with his flashlight he wanted to examine me. "You are the patient. So please take off your panties and I will examine you."

"I don't want to take off my panties, and I don't want to be the patient. So now you give me the flashlight and I will be the doctor!"

He was smart enough to know that the game would progress satisfactorily if he consented and gave me the flashlight.

"Open your mouth," I ordered.

He did, and *I* looked in, but the gaping mouth full of teeth was nothing new and certainly not very exciting. I was becoming bored and very hot under the heavy down comforter, when Kuba said, "If I show you mine, will you show me yours?"

"Show you what?"

"You know!"

I did not know! But the curiosity to find out what it was that I did not know was so strong that I couldn't resist, and on that fateful day I found out that mine was very different from his. Not knowing what to do with all this new information, slightly in awe of each other, we ended the game by putting on our pants and climbing out from under the covers.

My father found a job working for a Russian. I do not know in what capacity but I know that his law degree and the fact that he spoke and wrote fluent Russian and German were essential.

The first winter in Tarnopol seemed harsher than any I remembered in Krakow, but we were well equipped with food and coal, so all was well. There was not too much to complain about.

The changes crept up slowly. In spring, the Russian regime became more visible. Food was rationed and dwellings indiscriminately confiscated. We fell victim to the latter.

Very early one morning two men, one a commissar, knocked on the door. When the maid opened it, the elder one asked to speak to my uncle. "Comrade Kunstler! Are you Markus Kunstler?"

"Yes? What is this all about?" Uncle Motek asked.

"We are requisitioning your apartment!"

"What? What are you saying? What do you mean you're requisitioning?"

The commissar stepped into the hallway and opened a piece of paper, from which he read: "Apartment B, on the second floor of number three of Stanislawski Place, belonging to Markus Kunstler, will be vacated within twenty-four hours of personal possessions only. All furniture and bed linens are to remain for the commissar administrator of the third district . . ."

My uncle said, "But that's impossible! We are already two families living here, with children. Where are we going to go?"

"That, my dear Comrade Kunstler, is your problem. You have a sister living in the building; move in with her."

It was clear to all of us, who were now in the hallway listening to the Russian, that he meant business. All arguments were futile.

The commissar turned on his heels and left. When the door closed behind him, everyone was in shock.

"Philip, what do you think they are doing?" questioned Motek.

"They are moving more personnel into Poland."

"What are we going to do?"

"We arc going to move! Call Regina and tell her we have twenty-four hours to get out of this apartment."

And so, I was moving again. I was learning quickly that nothing was safe. Nothing was forever.

I was angry and very upset. My mother and Aunt Dziunia were both crying. My father tried to calm everyone. Reassuringly, he said, "Now, let's go and pack our stuff and take it to Regina's. We will have less space, but we will be together and there will be savings of food and coal. It is not the end of the world when you don't have a big apartment. So, go on. You children have to help also."

My mother was still moaning . . . my uncle wringing his hands. Obviously my father's speech had not helped any of them, and I was still furious.

An idea came into my head. I called Kuba into another room and instructed him. "Bring all the newspapers you can find."

Kuba came back with an armful.

"Now, we will take all the newspapers and shred them into tiny little squares. You know, like confetti."

"And then what?" Kuba couldn't understand what I had in mind. He looked confused.

I continued. "We will throw all these papers on the floor of the apartment and it will be so dirty that the Russians won't want it."

Kuba thought it was a brilliant idea, and we went to work cutting the paper.

✱ ✱ ✱

We were now all living in one room. My mother had nothing of her own, only her personal belongings, such as clothes and jewelry. We were very cramped for space. So the events that followed must have been rooted in her feelings of discomfort and loneliness.

One evening, when we were all in our beds—I was now privy to all of their conversations—my mother, thinking I was asleep, started crying and spoke to my father. "Philip, I heard about the new law that allows people to go back to the German-occupied area."

"Yes, I know. Joseph and Lola have already registered."

"Philip, I want to go home!"

"Look, Hela, I understand how you feel and I can't blame you, but my feelings about the Germans haven't changed."

"I know that, but maybe you were wrong. In their last letter, my parents said that life in Krakow was pretty normal and they were so glad they didn't come with us."

"Well, good for them! I'm glad they are happy."

"Look, Philip, things here are getting worse every day. Soldiers everywhere, impolite and uncivilized. They confiscate anything they want. They just come and take it! And there is nothing anyone can do about it."

"You are absolutely right. Things are not the best, but we have a war, and we are not starving."

"But so many of our friends are going back."

"I understand why they would want to go back, those doctors, lawyers, and professors. They are not working, but I am. So I don't need to go back and live under the Germans."

None of his arguments impressed her or changed her mind. She cried and cried and wanted to go home. So she registered, like all the others.

I don't know how much time passed, but before long I remember my father becoming suspicious about noises and sounds. The doors were being closed with latches and keys. When there was a knock or someone rang the bell, the adults in the house would look at one another, their eyes filled with terror.

And terror it was for me the night they came to take them.

Apparently, my father had been told by his boss that his name was on "the list." Those people whose names were on the list were being taken away in the middle of the night, without warning, and deported deep into the Soviet Union. All those doctors and lawyers and professors who wanted to go to the German side were being sent to Siberia.

Many of my father's friends had already been surprised. Some were found out in their hiding places, all deported in the same manner. Some were gone so many weeks that letters started coming back with descriptions that read like a horror story . . . living in the woods in barracks, not much food, doing very hard labor.

My parents went into hiding as soon as my father knew his name was on the list. They hid for weeks, sleeping in different places every night. Some days my aunt Regina took me for a visit to see them. I couldn't understand this new game of hiding. I was very upset. When my father saw me so unhappy, he explained and reassured me that this was temporary and that soon they would be home. He swore me to absolute secrecy as to their whereabouts.

They must have been doing this for at least two months when, one day, they came home and said that they believed the danger had passed and they were safe again, here in our house. In the middle of that same night, there was a loud knocking, and a thunderous voice commanded us to open the door. Sure enough, it was happening. They were coming to take us!

The coincidence was enormous—that it was that night, the night my parents came home. Had someone denounced them, or had the house been under constant surveillance?

Suddenly, the door to our bedroom swung open, and two men pushing their way in shouted, "Are you Dr. Philip Kunstler?"

"Yes, I am."

"And this is your wife, Helena, and your daughter?" he asked, pointing his finger in my direction.

My father looked straight at me and said, "No, this is not my daughter. She is my sister's child." Seeing my aunt Regina in the doorway, he motioned to her and said, "Put her to bed. Please, Regina, this is no time for children to stand around."

I am standing silently, my head pressed into my aunt's stomach, glancing sideways at this strange scene. I am so afraid and the fear is closing my throat . . . I can't swallow . . . in the pit of my stomach a sharp pain . . . . my heart will soon rip open my chest and jump out of my skin and I will be dead and I will not feel this terror that is paralyzing me now.

I know what is happening but I don't want to believe it.

My father has some words with the officer, my mother is packing in silence, and then he goes to help her.

What does this mean, I'm not his daughter? He must be playing another pretending game.

My aunt is dripping warm tears. They fall on my neck. She is holding me too tight, pressing my cheek to her soft, warm abdomen. My father holds us both for a moment and then they yank him away. My mother kisses my head. She is sobbing.

The door closes with a thud. They are gone. And I am left alone . . . ! They went away and left me!

Aunt Regina says she has seen my father. He is in a railroad car under one of the bridges. He can be seen. She wants to take me there. I don't understand very well why he is in a railroad car, but I want to go. I want to see my father!

Regina is crying. She says, "Don't be afraid when you see him. He has changed."

We go to the bridge that spans hundreds of rails. There are trains on some of the tracks. She points to the freight train just below the bridge. "That car! The one with the circle on it. See the little window just to the right of the circle?"

"Yes, I see it."

"Now you look there and I will call him." She calls, "Philip! Philip!"

I can see the head of a man coming out of the small narrow window at the very top of the car.

His hair is almost white.

He turns and I see it's my father.

I can't believe what I see. What did he do to his hair? He looks so different. He calls out to me. I wave . . . he sends me a kiss . . . I throw kisses with both my hands. I want to get down there to the train, but my aunt is holding me tight. My eyes are blurred by tears. I hear steps. The sound is distorted, wavy. The soldiers shout. They tell us to get off the bridge.

On the way home, in the tram, Aunt Regina explains what has happened. She tells me that sometimes people become gray overnight, when something shocking has happened to them. I hear her only vaguely. The voice in my head is louder. It obliterates her words. "Why did he leave me? Why is his hair all white? Is all this possible?" I am in shock. *Will the same thing happen to me?* I wonder.

When we return home from the bridge, everyone is waiting.

"Did you see him?"

"Yes, we saw him. He looks all right. Just the hair makes him seem different. He waved to us. He saw the child; that was the most important thing."

The apartment is full of people. Everyone wants to touch me. Today I am the center of their attention. They are overwhelming me and I want to hide.

I run to my oldest cousin, Henryk. He has been away at the University in Lwow and now he is back, sitting on the couch, talking to Kuba. He picks me up and sits me on his lap. I love him. He is so tall and so handsome, a mop of curly black hair with one corkscrew curl always hanging down on his forehead. I am his favorite girl, he tells me. His love for me is very, very special. I wrap my arms around his neck. He strokes my hair and calls me his "golden butterfly."

I am sitting on his lap, holding on. I don't feel safe anymore. I bury my face in his neck, but the smell is different. The feel is different. Nothing is the same . . .

I wonder what will happen to me now . . .

It's like a dream. Everything is vague. I am ill, some sort of fever. I am in bed . . . and I have visitors . . . I hear them through a fog . . . they are asking me questions. I can't respond. I have no voice.

Time passes and I am not within it. I am neither here nor there. It's evening again. The lamp on the nightstand throws a dim glow on the bed. The rest of the room is darkness. I can't see . . . I hear old Mrs. Pins, the dentist's wife, who is always very jovial, now serious and concerned.

She asks, "Regina, why hasn't she cried? Any child would cry if her parents were taken away! She hasn't shed a tear. Why? Maybe if you put some onion slices to her forehead that would make her cry. It will be good for her."

Why does Mrs. Pins want me to cry? I don't understand.

I don't understand what is going on. Why is everyone whispering around me? I open my eyes. It's daytime. There are flowers in the vase. My cousin, Henryk, is holding my hand and kissing my forehead. I thought he was still in Lwow . . .

I am looking out the window. The pigeons on the windowsill are pecking at something. They are almost in the room. I look at them. Their heads dart with jerky little movements. I can't move mine.

More time passes, until one day I see the sun streaming through the curtains, and I am hungry. All of a sudden I want to eat bread and butter. I sit up in bed. My aunt Regina brings dark bread thickly spread with butter, watches me eat, and then hugs and kisses me over and over. There are always tears on her cheeks.

CHAPTER 4

Parents Gone;
Learning to Live without Them

At home every day . . . I don't go to dancing school anymore. Maybe it isn't safe. Maybe I haven't recovered completely from the illness.

Aunt Regina teaches me to knit. I sit by her in her workroom, where the big knitting machine is standing. I want to help her but she will not let me touch the machine. She says it's dangerous; I could cut off a finger.

She is mothering me. She tells me I must learn to knit by hand, with knitting needles, so I can make sweaters for my children. I like that, the thought that I will be a mother and have my own children.

My cousin, Henryk, has gone back to Lwow. His brother, Tushek, doesn't let me out of his sight. He loves to tease me. We push and pull a lot. We play rough. He throws me in the air and then catches me just in the nick of time. I like to be with him. He carries me on his shoulders and makes me feel endangered all the time. There is an air of excitement when I am with him, and I forget everything else.

Tushek is a clown by nature. Everything he does is funny. Everybody loves him. He has a clubfoot and walks with a limp, but it doesn't matter; no one pays attention to his deformity. His hair is bright red and curly, and his face looks like it belongs on a circus poster. He is the most sensitive member of my family. He knows how I feel even when he doesn't ask me. Tushek talks funny; he turns and twists the language. He even makes up words. He turns everything into a joke, but when he talks to me his tone is serious. Only his eyes are always smiling.

He told me once that he knows how I feel not having my mother and father. He knows it well because his father died when he was just a boy, and since then there was only he and Henryk and their mother, my Aunt Regina.

Tushek adores his mother. There is no doubt about that.

I often wonder if having a clubfoot makes him so special.

He has three very close friends, Marek, Teddy, and Mooha Pins. They live downstairs, one floor below us. They are all about Tushek's age. Marek and Teddy go to school. They wear *casquettes*, navy blazers with an emblem on one pocket, and have turquoise piping on the side seams of their trousers. Mooha goes to music school. She plays the piano. She looks funny because she's too tall for a girl. All three of them are giants, like Dr. Pins.

Tushek and Marek, the oldest of the three, are inseparable. We all spend a lot of time together. Now that I am part of their group *I* feel grown up. They treat me like their mascot. Sometimes Mooha and I do what only girls do. She paints my nails and fusses with my hair, designing a new hairdo, totally unsuitable for a little girl. Mooha's own hair is dark and very thick and very straight. She wears it cut Chinese style, and of course can do absolutely nothing with it.

One day I find a lipstick and paint my mouth red. Mooha lets me dress up in her clothes and builds me into them with safety pins. She perches a hat on my head, gloves on my hands, and sends me to show the boys.

I shuffle very slowly down the hallway. My feet are so small they don't even fill the toes of Mooha's shoes. But I must have high heels to complete my fashion-model image.

I stand in the doorway where the boys are playing chess.

"Hmm, huh, huh"—a little cough to let them know I'm there. They look in my direction.

Tushek whispers loudly, "Do you see what I see? Don't look now. She mustn't know we are looking at her!"

"Who?"

"That exquisite creature standing behind us!"

Marek looks in my direction. "Oh, yes, she is incredibly beautiful."

"Do you know who she is?"

"No, but I suppose some famous actress, or maybe a princess."

"Excuse me, Madame, are you an actress or a princess? My friend here would like to know."

Marek takes my hand and kisses the glove.

I am in the game. "Of course I am a princess, kind sir. I've come from the land of the purple strawberries, to find a suitable suitor. Would you know of any?"

"Well, a suitable suitor for such a beautiful beauty as you? That will be a most difficult task."

"Ah! But to him who finds me a suitor, I will give a white stallion and a castle on a hill and jewels like no man has ever seen before, because they are only mined in my kingdom."

"We will find you a suitable suitor, but first we must find out if you are a suitable princess."

We all burst out laughing. Tushek plunks a kiss on my forehead, turns me around, and with a pat on my behind sends me back down the hall to play with Mooha.

Kuba is jealous. He is not always included. But he is a child! I am special!

Kuba says, "No! That's not true."

But everybody treats me special. After all, I have no mommy or daddy.

My aunt Regina receives a letter from my father. She reads it and cries. But she tells me they are fine. She reads aloud the part addressed to me. Oh, my goodness, I am so happy. Daddy wrote me a letter! Maybe they will come back for me soon.

I think about my parents . . . I don't remember them so well anymore—just my father, the day on the bridge. I miss them anyway. I feel strange again, to be the only one like that, with no parents at all. I am sad. Tushek tries to lift my spirits by inventing a new game that will become my most favorite pastime for a while—he builds me a tower out of chairs. There are chairs on top of chairs, on top of boards piled on top of more chairs.

It is a maze of rungs, going up and sideways, and landings where I sit on the way up to the ceiling—for that is the ultimate goal—to be able to touch the ceiling. I feel like I've conquered a mountain. I am the queen looking down on my subjects! I command from up there, and unless I give permission, no one can climb up behind me.

I am untouchable! I have great power!

Tushek indulges me, of course, and I see he is pleased that this game absorbs me so completely. Kuba, on the other hand, again feels very slighted and angry. He doesn't like my illusions of grandeur and complains. Sometimes I let him come with me up the tower. We hang towels and blankets and make hideaways. I relinquish some of my exclusive ownership, realizing that I need Kuba to play with me.

The ceiling is full of handprints. Getting to the top is no longer interesting. We know how to do it with blindfolds. We invent a new game. We play war. We hide. We make warlike noises. We peek from holes! We fall!

Aunt Regina and Kuba's mother, Aunt Dziunia, are appalled when they surprise us during an action-filled moment, where Kuba is wounded and falls limp to the ground. We are both like monkeys on this scaffold. We can fool them! They think he is hurt, but he gets up, laughing. His mother doesn't think it's funny, but Regina is visibly relieved.

She walks off, muttering, "I have to talk to Tushek not to erect that catafalque again."

Tushek is so agile that he walks on the parapet of the roof of our building to free a dove that is caught in some wire. People in the square below shout with horror. A woman faints! Those who know him don't pay any attention at all. They know he won't fall. He could be a high-wire artist. He teaches me balance.

We climb trees in the park. I stand on his shoulders, jump with ease to the ground, and then pirouette down the grassy slope. I like to swing from the high branches. Sometimes he leaves me there and walks away. I am afraid to let go. It looks too far to the ground. I plead with him. "Please come back and take me down."

"No. You do it yourself."

He encourages me to jump. He's there, waiting for me under the tree. I let go and land on my feet like an acrobat.

"You see! You can do it!"

Tushek teaches me not to be afraid!

Aunt Regina has established a correspondence with my Uncle Mooniu in Krakow. He has news of my parents through a businessman and friend, Mr. Weiss, who lives in Sweden. Sweden is neutral. He can send parcels to the deported political prisoners held in Siberia. We get letters also from my father and my mother. I wait for the mailman and look at all the letters that come to our house. I can only read capital letters, but I recognize my father's handwriting.

CHAPTER 5

Going to Zloczow
to Visit Kuba's Grandma

It had to be summer now, because it was very hot again. I loved going to the factory for fresh *makagigi*, a square candy made of honey and walnuts. But now it was too hot in the factory, with all those kettles boiling. So Uncle Motek brought the ice cream and candy home to us.

Aunt Dziunia decided to visit her mother. She was taking Kuba. I was invited to go with them. I was hesitant to leave Aunt Regina, but Kuba pleaded, he wanted me to come. I let myself be convinced and very quickly became involved with the excitement of a journey to Zloczow.

It was not too far away, just a few hours by train. We left early for the train station, this time in a real taxi. The train ride was rather uneventful. I remember sitting by the window in the compartment that we had all to ourselves. It was a plush compartment, with dark, red-velvet seats and little lace doilies where the head rests. We had sandwiches, fruit, and cookies, and before long the conductor announced that in five minutes we would be in Zloczow.

Aunt Dziunia spotted her mother and her brother, Jakob, on the platform, who were intensely following the windows of the train, looking for us. She waved with both arms, her body half out of the window. As soon as her mother saw her, she ran on the platform, following the train until it came to a complete stop. With her arms outstretched, she helped Kuba and me down the steep steps of the rail car.

Everybody hugged everybody! I was introduced to Grandma Rachel, who was so pleased to see us that as soon as the bags were in the carriage outside the station, she took me and Kuba by the hand, right to the ice cream vendor on the other side of the street. Meanwhile Aunt Dziunia huddled in conversation with her brother, Jakob.

The station was in the center of town. From there till the outskirts stretched a wide avenue lined with enormous chestnut trees.

While we drove down the avenue, Uncle Jakob sat opposite me, observing me all the time without saying a word. He impressed me immediately with his size. I was a little scared of him. His black eyes looked right into my soul. He was definitely not your everyday, run-of-the-mill Jewish family man. I am assuming that he was younger than my father, and he must have shaved his head, for there wasn't a hair on it.

I sat there looking through and around him, afraid to meet his eyes. I noticed his jacket was twice as wide at the shoulders as any other that I had ever seen. He looked very strong. (Later I found out he had been a boxer.)

Someone was pulling at my sleeve to get me out of my reverie. I turned my head and Grandma Rachel gently took my chin in her cupped hand. Smiling, she asked, "And what were you thinking about?"

The cab stopped in front of a very beautiful building. On the ground floor were two stores, between them a large portal through which we entered the building.

The driver, Uncle Jakob, and a youth who appeared out of nowhere brought our luggage upstairs.

The apartment was on the second floor, very large and sunny, and full of delicious smells—foretelling a fabulous dinner for my ravenously hungry stomach.

Everything was strange to me. Here I knew no one and nothing about the family and Kuba knew everybody!

As she was setting the table, the cook was bombarding Kuba with all kinds of questions. He was obviously an adored child in his grandmother's house. The only grandson, and everyone spoiled him.

I followed him around like a shadow, peeking into rooms, looking for Uncle Jakob. He had disappeared. When I finally mustered the courage to ask where he was, everyone looked at me with surprise.

"Oh, you didn't know? He is downstairs in the store."

"He has a store downstairs?"

"Yes, we have the jewelry store. Didn't you see it when we arrived?"

Grandma Rachel reached behind her for the receiver that hung on the wall and pressed a buzzer.

"Jakob, dinner is on the table and the children are starving, so come right up."

Moments later someone was running up the old wooden stairs. I heard the door open and close. He came in! I listened to his footsteps, muffled by the heavy Persian rug in the entry hall. Uncle Jakob was washing his hands, as was done ritually for centuries in every Jewish home before eating.

I waited for him to come and sit with us at the table. He intimidated me and made me curious and excited at the same time.

His shaved head was shining. His eyes were smiling and he had an expression of amusement on his face. He was aware of my shyness and tried to draw me out with some funny stories. His physical appearance was like nothing I had ever seen before. His shoulders and neck were enormous, and now that he was in shirtsleeves, one could see the bulging muscles of his upper arms.

All of a sudden I realized what it was that had me so mesmerized. Uncle Jakob looked exactly like a hero in one of the comic strips my father and I used to read on Sunday mornings.

I burst out laughing and said, "You look like the hero of the 'Pat and Patachon' comic strip in the Sunday paper."

Everyone laughed and I was very much at ease now.

The summer heat continued. Aunt Dziunia, Kuba, and I went frequently to the woods with a picnic basket. Once I went with Uncle Jakob to a soccer game and loved it, but Kuba did not want to go. The rest of the time we spent in the store.

Almost every day our meals were interrupted by the loud shriek of an air-raid siren. These were practice runs, and we would hurriedly proceed to the cellar, careful not to panic or trip anyone on the stairs. Down in the basement there were provisions of food and water, flashlights, and blankets. Everyone had an assigned place to go, so that the person in charge could take count to make sure no one was missing.

Uncle Jakob was the air-raid warden. He gave sharp, clear instructions and everyone obeyed.

It happened, as he had predicted, just before dawn—sirens announcing the bombers. We descended into the shelter and sat waiting for the all-clear. For a while there was silence, and then the inimitable sound of bombs exploding all around us, above ground.

The cellar shook and reverberated with every explosion, close or far away. All of a sudden the lights went out! No more electricity. The tense silence was punctuated with frightened gasps.

The war was back! Right over our heads!

Some children cried, but I wasn't one of them. I had heard bombs before.

Uncle Jakob's flashlight pierced the total darkness. The small beam of light was reassuring. Calmly, he gave us the first instructions. "It looks like we will be here for a while. Who knows how long the raid will last? We have everything we need. Do not use your flashlights unnecessarily." He was in charge. "Light two candles, one at each end of the cellar."

After the candles were lit, everyone felt better.

I became aware of the musty, damp smell of the cellar, and I thought, *I don't like it underground—I hope we don't have to stay here for long.*

The pounding of the bombs and mortars didn't cease for what seemed like hours. Soon the conversations became more normal.

Some of the men, wearing armbands, were with the civil defense. They had authority and we felt safe with them around.

We must have been in the cellar for hours when a strange sound shook the building. Some moments later someone started pounding on the metal door, yelling, "People! People! Are there people down there? Come on out, quick! Your building was hit! It's burning! You will all be burned alive!"

Uncle Jakob ran up the stairs four at a time. Some of the men with armbands followed, and some helped us leave the cellar as quickly as possible.

There was no panic.

Now that we were on the sidewalk, the building didn't look so bad at all. There was some damage on one side, but the rest was still standing. Many of the other buildings across the street and around us were burning or were partly destroyed.

Aunt Dziunia was scared. She held Kuba and me by the hand, looking up at the apartment where we lived.

"Do you think we should try to go upstairs?" she asked her mother.

Grandma Rachel looked up, and as the people were milling around the front of the building, she couldn't see if there was any fire there. So she moved closer to the open door and went in.

I pulled my hand from Dziunia's grip and ran in behind her. "I'm going with you!" I am energized by the danger of being in a burning building.

Grandma Rachel climbed the stairs so fast I could hardly keep up with her.

When we entered the apartment she went directly to the fireplace. This fireplace was not like most fireplaces. It was in the shape of a tall cube, reaching from floor to ceiling. Two of its sides were covered with beautiful ceramic tiles, stamped with various patterns, and glazed in light blue like the rest of the decor in the room.

On one side, about two feet from the floor, there was a small iron door that covered the hearth. The whole structure sat about six inches from the walls, and in that space, wood was stored so it would be dry and ready for use.

It was precisely behind this firewood that Grandma Rachel had hidden part of the inventory of the jewelry store. She started pulling out the wood. When all of it was out, she got on her knees, and reaching way in the back, pulled out a bundle tied in a linen handkerchief, and then another and another.

Her arm was in that space between the chimney and wall, and she was pushing her shoulder in, trying to get whatever it was she couldn't reach, when she turned to me. "You try," she said. "You are small and thin; maybe you'll be able to reach it."

She got up and stepped away. I pushed almost half of my body between the chimney and the wall, trying in vain to get that last bundle. Every time I thought I had it, I couldn't hold on to it because it was so heavy it would slip through my fingers.

Once more—oh, here, I got it now! It sure was heavy, and I knew there were jewels inside. I could feel the rings through the fabric.

With pride, I said, "I got it! I got it out, Grandma!" When she didn't answer, I looked around—she wasn't there. Apparently, Grandma had gone to fetch Jakob so he would retrieve the bundle that neither she nor I had been able to reach. With the jewelry in my hand, I ran out of the apartment.

On the landing, I stopped dead in my tracks. Oh, my God! There are no stairs! Only a big hole where the stairs had been.

What do I do now?

My heart started pounding. I was so scared. My knees were shaking. I went back to the apartment. I had never been so afraid in my whole life.

I leaned out the window and tried to shout, but only a very thin, shaky voice came out. "Help"—I force the little voice out. "Help." I wave my arms.

Someone on the street noticed me. The crowd below, on the sidewalk, became agitated. "Someone get her down! Get her down!"

More yelling and shouting. Suddenly two hands grabbed me by the shoulders. This man had been in the adjacent apartment, throwing some of his possessions out the window.

He took me with him next door and began explaining to me, "I will throw out all the bedding and all the clothes and mattresses from both apartments, and then we will jump."

When all of that was done, he said, "Don't be afraid. I will hold you and protect you with my body."

He first sat on the windowsill and swung his legs over. Then he turned and slowly lifted me onto his lap. He surrounded me with his body and wrapped his arms around, holding me very tight. He jumped.

Seconds later, we were on the pile below, both in one piece, not one bone broken.

I felt saved. I was so happy to be on the ground.

I handed Grandma Rachel the bundle that I had held tight in my hand during this whole drama.

In the middle of that night we left town and went to stay at the home of one of our grandma's friends. It was there that we lived for the next few weeks, while the incoming conquerors settled in.

CHAPTER 6

The War Is Following Me

Almost immediately the Germans plastered the town with all kinds of edicts. The day after they came into Zloczow, all the able-bodied men were assembled and put to work digging ditches. These were foxholes for the German soldiers, and everyone had to report to work.

Some men were afraid to report and decided to hide. Forced labor meant lost freedom. The Germans promised the townspeople enormous rewards for denouncing anyone who disobeyed their orders.

There were Ukrainians who awaited the Germans with great impatience. They were ready to serve the Reich and themselves at the same time.

One of the first incidents of denunciation that I witnessed with horror was when the Gestapo came to the home of our neighbor, a young man someone had denounced. He was an invalid with a deformed and withered hand, and one leg shorter than the other. He sat on his doorstep, and with a sad smile pointed to his hand, which was very small and almost folded at the wrist. He said to them, showing his hand, "I cannot hold a shovel. That is why I didn't go to work."

He thought, of course, they would leave him alone. He wasn't afraid. After all, everyone who had eyes could see that he couldn't hold anything. What would they want with him, anyway?

The Gestapo officer unbuttoned his shiny leather holster and slowly removed his Lugar. The young man's eyes widened as he understood what was about to happen. He tried to say something. He opened his mouth. The bullet pierced his forehead so precisely and accurately that he slumped to the ground with a jerk and fell like a rumpled doll in front of the step he had been sitting on.

I was in the side yard pulling out young carrots for soup. The whole thing took but a minute, or maybe two. I did not understand. Nothing had ever changed so drastically from a living, moving, smiling person to this heap that lay on the doorstep! Never, right there in front of my very own eyes. Never before!

I knew that it was useless what his mother was doing. Instinct told me. Her arms were still outstretched . . . she wanted to say something to the Gestapo man, but it all happened so quickly . . . . Her arms were still outstretched and her mouth was open when her son fell to the ground and became a heap! She took him in her arms, and, sitting on the step, began to lament. The uncontrolled expression of her grief frightened me. She was talking to him and I knew he didn't hear. She was stroking his hair and telling him the story, how she was sure they would leave him alone when they saw his infirmity. She couldn't understand what they wanted from him. Didn't they see he couldn't work with his hand so badly crippled?

Now people were trying to take the dead body of the sweet innocent cripple from the arms of his grief-stricken mother. She didn't want to let them take him. She was holding on, telling them again and again how she didn't understand what the Germans wanted.

Suddenly, a middle-aged man came through the crowd and knelt by the mother. "He is dead, Sarah. We have to bury him."

All at once she stopped talking and raised her brow in an expression of understanding and acceptance. She let go of the body and they took him away.

And here I was, having witnessed again the passage from life into death, wiser, no longer having to wonder what it meant. I had known him only moments before—alive—and now I knew him dead. But I was not afraid of death or the dead man. Just the Gestapo man—his cruel eyes, his gloved hands, and his blindingly polished boots.

(In Los Angeles, maybe twenty years later, I was on my way to a funeral, very upset, when I lost my way and made an illegal left turn. The officer who stopped me and asked for my license never understood the hysterical reaction I had when I first saw his shiny black-leather boots.)

That first day, terror was very generously dispensed. The killing of Bernard, the cripple, was not the only incident I saw. In the house down the road lived an old man I knew. He had a beard and side locks and was dressed in a long black silk coat; obviously he was a Hassid. He must have thought he was too old to go to work. The same group that had come for Bernard went to pay him a visit. The poor man was hiding in an outhouse in the back garden. There was a fissure under the door and his black shoes and white socks could be seen through it. I don't think they even bothered to call his name. The machine gun unleashed a string of bullets that pierced the wood and made little holes right through the middle of the toilet. Blood trickled out under the door.

That same day, another man was brutally killed while working in the trenches. The German guard split his head in two with the man's own shovel.

Fear was gripping everyone. People talked in whispers about how the Germans managed to impose their will with such lightning speed. Some people knew more than others.

I kept asking my aunt, "When are we going home?" I thought home, in Tarnopol, would be better. Of course there, nobody was killing anybody (or so I thought).

My Aunt Dziunia started acting as if she was crazy, hysterically crying, wringing her hands. I didn't know why, so I asked her what was wrong. She told me she was afraid that she would never again see Uncle Motek, her husband. At the moment there was no way to get back to Tarnopol. Maybe there was no transportation. Most likely the authorities wouldn't allow anyone to travel.

I remember Dziunia being discouraged by her brother against leaving. He was worried about the danger of a woman traveling alone with two small children. We were again in a state of war, her brother argued.

"Dziunia, wait. Don't go now. Wait a few days longer. It's too dangerous to travel now!"

"Jakob, you must know how I feel. Look at what has happened in just a few days. I am so afraid I will not see Motek again. I must go! I don't understand what is going on now; people are being taken away and they don't come back. Some are shot and killed without reason. What if they take Motek and send him to work somewhere and I don't know where he is?"

Jakob agreed, but he said, "In a few days we will know better the situation with the Germans. You have to think of the children. A woman alone with two small children . . . too dangerous!"

The discussion continued way into the night. We were sent off to sleep, Kuba and I, but while Kuba fell asleep instantly I listened through the door until the voices were still.

A few days later, one morning, Aunt Dziunia came out of her room looking very different. She was dressed to the teeth in a most elegant dress, white shoes, and a little white hat coquettishly perched on her right eye. She looked very excited, as if she were going to do something secret and forbidden. One last look in the mirror, and then with a wink she turned and went out the door.

I was terribly curious, so I asked Grandma Rachel where Aunt Dziunia was going. No one wanted to tell me. There was a strange note in all of this. Here, people are killed, everyone is in a state of shock, and my aunt gets all dressed up and leaves the house as if she were going to a clandestine rendezvous. There was one thing I thought very strange: when she was putting on her hat just before she left, her hands were trembling.

Aunt Dziunia was quite young at that time, in her late twenties or maybe early thirties. She is an attractive person. Her face is round and her coloring rather fair, with blonde hair and blue eyes. She looks like the girls you see in old paintings tending to sheep or geese. Her hair is cut short and curled with a wave over one eye. She is a bit round of body and not very tall but always wears very high heels that give her an air of self-assurance, which in stocking feet would have been difficult to achieve. (I have seen the same look come into the eyes of little girls who finally master the art of walking in their mother's high-heeled shoes.) If you looked at her then, you could not tell—what I later learned was one's best asset for survival—that Aunt Dziunia was Jewish.

She didn't listen to anybody, and with her womanly instinct and some fantastic fabrications she went to the German commandatur to ask for a special permission to travel with her two young children to Tarnopol.

When she walked through the door waving in her hand the piece of paper no one believed she could obtain, there was a definite look of triumph in her eyes.

As much as I wanted to go back to Tarnopol, now that we were going I didn't want to leave. I couldn't understand what I felt. I sat on the chair in the large entry hall and cried quietly. I didn't want anyone to know; only the tears flowing on my cheeks like torrents were betraying me.

Uncle Jakob came over to me, and picking me up out of the chair, sat down himself, seating me on his lap and holding my head gently on his shoulder.

He whispered, "Now, now. I know how you feel."

As he said that, I stopped crying and asked myself how he knew what I felt. One thing for sure, now I felt better . . . now that he held me and I felt his arms surround me, I felt infinitely better.

In Tarnopol everyone was safe, but everything was different. We had left a Russian Tarnopol and come back to a German Tarnopol. There was a sense of danger everywhere.

My Uncle Motek went to the factory as always, but I no longer had a ballet school to go to. My teacher had been a Russian ballerina, so she was gone. We were not allowed to go anywhere we wanted. We had to stay in certain parts of the city. This was while they built the fence that would enclose the ghetto of Tarnopol.

The transition from freedom to ghetto life was swift. Many people who I did not know came to live in our building. Probably all those who were not Jewish moved out and the Jews from all the other parts of the city moved in.

In the ghetto, the first winter was painful. We had to stand in interminable lines for food and anything else we needed.

Aunt Regina has been supporting herself since the death of her husband by making knitwear with a knitting machine. There are plenty of leftover yarns with which she makes clothing for herself, for me, and for Tushek.

Before the bitter winter cold, even during the fall when the rains began I wore my sandals with rubber galoshes. But for winter I needed shoes, and my aunt couldn't find any in the ghetto. I remember going to someone's house, where used clothes and shoes were sold in hiding. Everything was now being done clandestinely. Aunt Regina looked and looked, but among all the children's shoes for sale there were none that fit me.

I stayed home most of the time, sitting next to my aunt and the machine, tying pieces of yarn and winding them into balls, from which she would make sweaters, mufflers, hats, and even gloves.

My aunt was still in business, so many people came to see her. Everyone would bring bits of information or question her about what she knew.

Mrs. Pins asked one day, "Did you know Sonia and Ronek left the ghetto? This morning, Mania, their neighbor, went over and they were gone. Their apartment empty!"

Sometimes there were clear signs that the Germans took them, and sometimes the grapevine would bring back news that they were safe on the "other side." This was now a new terminology that came into usage. The "other side" meant outside the ghetto, probably in a different town or city, and, of course, with forged identity papers, which were referred to as "Aryan papers" because they always contained a baptismal certificate—"proof" that one was not a Jew.

My aunt no longer allowed me to go out into the street because one day I saw a pregnant woman standing in line for bread that had a malaise and fainted. A German officer was trying to bring order to the line. He walked over and sliced her belly open. I squeezed my eyes shut so tightly they hurt. I thought I never wanted to see again. Never! I wanted to be blind!

I threw up in the dark, my eyes squeezed shut, my aunt holding my head. When I stopped retching she wiped my mouth with a handkerchief, and without a word we went home. She prepared a hot tub of water, washed me lovingly, and she cried.

CHAPTER 7

The Germans
Chased out the Russians

It must have been around that time that they decided to have me leave the ghetto.

How they made the arrangements I do not know . . . probably not by direct mail, but letters were coming and Aunt Regina was making feverish preparations for something. Everything was secret; we children had gotten used to that. Not much was said. Looks and motions had new meanings and had to be interpreted like a new language.

At the time my parents were deported we were living in Tarnopol under Russian occupation, and my grandparents and uncle were still in Slomniki, under the Germans. My mother had written frequently and received many letters from her family. There was always joy and excitement when a letter arrived from the other side. I liked to examine the envelopes, because the stamps were always very colorful. Now I waited for my aunt to finish reading and tell me about the letters. With time, I learned to recognize the handwriting of my grandparents and uncle.

Even though my parents were gone, the letters continued to come. Regina would always tell me that one or the other had written asking about me, or sharing some news about my mother and father. I sensed a difference in the way Regina opened the letters. Now she tore them open feverishly, and while reading would steal a look in my direction. I knew that the content of those letters had something to do with me, but she never told me anything, only that Mooniu was well and was sending his love. I thought, *she thinks I don't know, but I know something is going on.*

She didn't leave me much time to think about or to feel the pain of leaving her and the rest of the family. She told me I was going to spend a little time with my grandparents, where things were better because they were not in the ghetto. But I knew what that meant. She had prepared everything I would wear . . . my blue wool winter coat with the gray curly lamb collar and cuffs, and the hat that went with it.

I loved that coat when it was new—long, long ago—when I had parents and I was just like any other child. I even remember when the box arrived from the furrier. I couldn't believe my eyes! All that fur! That beautiful, soft, curly lamb . . .

Now the fur was flat, yellowed, very worn. The sleeves had been lengthened with some other blue material. You could see the difference in color where the side seams and the hem had been let out to the last centimeter.

Aunt Regina was *dressing* me, not *helping* me dress. She made me stand before her, and starting with the undershirt, she proceeded to lovingly dress me like you would a baby, not letting me do anything. I couldn't understand why she wouldn't let me dress myself. But she wouldn't! And as she slipped one garment on top of the other, tears were running down her cheeks. She never said a word and continued dressing me as if she were performing some sacred ritual. After I was all bundled up, she hugged me. Tushek picked me up and took me down the stairs, carrying me in his arms.

Out on the street the cold wind hit my face. Tushek put me down and wrapped my chin with the long, multicolored muffler Aunt Regina made for my trip. He hugged me and kissed me as he always did, starting with my forehead, and then both eyes, the tip of my nose, my mouth, and finally my chin. When that was done he recited some very magic words, which started with "Abracadabra," took off my gloves, and while kissing every one of my ten fingers, pronounced all kinds of favorable omens for my trip. By the time he finished I was in stitches and couldn't catch my breath. It was then that he turned and walked away.

I was still laughing when my aunt took me by the hand and led me to the gate—the only way out of the ghetto. She stopped about a hundred yards from there. She crouched to my level. We embraced. Then she motioned with her head to the open gate, and said "Go. Just go right through and don't stop for anything. Don't turn around to look at me. When you are out on the other side of the gate, turn right and don't stop. Keep on going. There will be a man who will take your hand. Don't say anything until you are well out of earshot. He will take you to your grandparents. He's waiting, so go! And God be with you."

She kissed me, and, turning me to face the gate, she gave me a little shove.

I went straight to the gate with a steady step, right through. Nothing to it! My heart was pounding so hard I thought the German guard would surely hear it. He looked at me, smiled, and I went past him, turned right . . . soon a man took my hand and we went down the road.

Everything is white. Snow had fallen during the night and only the center part of the road had wheel tracks on it . . . not many footsteps on the sidewalk . . . not many people walked around the ghetto wall. We walked straight, until the street turned into a country road. I didn't say a word and neither did he. I looked ahead and walked.

The sun is shining but it's very cold. Soon my feet felt like they were frozen. My right hand was warm, but my left I could hardly feel at all. I tried to move my fingers. They were completely numb. Then a thought came to me! I pulled my right hand out of the man's grip and ran around him to the other side, so he was holding my left hand and warming it a little.

Now I dared look at him. He was enormous. Not heavy or broad, but very, very tall. I stole a glance behind me. No more walls! No more ghetto! I thought *this means I am free. I am out and no one is after us. We are safe.*

I pulled my hand out of his and tugged at his sleeve. "What is your name?" I asked, looking up. I'm not a bit afraid of this giant, who looks back down at me and smiles.

"I am Wladek! I worked for many years for your grandfather, David Spira, in the warehouse. Do you remember me? I recognized you right away. Now I work for your Uncle Mooniu. He sent me for you. We are going to Slomniki, where your grandparents are still residing. While we are traveling I am supposed to be your uncle."

My mind flooded with memories of my parents and grandparents. I caught myself thinking maybe my parents would be there also. I wished for a miracle. Maybe the omens

Tushek had conjured up would all come true, and what had happened in Tarnopol would turn out to be a nightmare . . . only a nightmare.

Wladek's voice brought me back to reality. "Are you cold?"

"My feet are numb and so are my hands."

He stood in place. After knocking one foot against the other to shake off the snow, he stomped up and down. "Do like me and your feet will not be so cold."

He took my hands and cupped them in front of his mouth and then blew hot breath on them, warming them a little. "About two more kilometers until the inn where we will spend the night. Do you think you can walk, or do you want to ride on my back?"

Who does he think I am? A little ninny? A weak little girl? If he can walk, I can walk! I said, "We should both walk. We will get to the inn much faster."

The sun has set and night was falling quickly. We had been walking for hours. I was feeling close to tears when we arrived at the inn.

Wladek helped me take off my coat and gloves. My hands were totally useless. I could do nothing with them. There was an open fireplace in the room, and we both stood in front, warming our frozen bodies. Slowly, I started feeling my hands and feet. My fingers and toes were hurting . . . feeling was coming back with excruciating pain. I cried silently.

The innkeeper's wife, certainly a mother herself, noticed my tears, and right away, trying to console me, took me by the hand. "You poor darling child," she said, "you must have been frozen. I will heat some water and prepare a bath that will make you feel better. Where are you people coming from anyway?"

She turned to Wladek, who, looking confused, was not going to let me out of his sight. He started saying something, and I interrupted him. "It will be all right. I will be a very good girl and will behave very nicely. You need not worry, 'Uncle'!"

Wladek was a peasant with a heart of gold, and his loyalty to my family was absolutely without question. My uncle trusted him with my life. I later found out that Wladek could do anything; sometimes he was entrusted with the most dangerous tasks. Now I sensed that he was at a loss for words, but I knew he understood what I said. He could trust me.

The woman took me to the back room. She poured the boiling water into a small tin tub. Then, from the courtyard she brought a bucket of cold water and added a little to the hot. She let me undress alone and waited for me to get into the tub.

"The warm water is very good for frostbitten hands," she said as she rubbed my hands and feet while I sat in the water.

I felt my body warming, and it felt so good to be in this warm water, so relaxing, so soothing.

I must have closed my eyes, for she said to me, "Now is not the time to sleep. I must go back to help my husband serve the food, so here is a towel. Dry yourself and come back to the table."

She handed me a towel that felt like sandpaper. It was hard and rough, but it dried me very well. I dressed myself and came back into the room where Wladek was waiting.

My cheeks were so red that he laughed. He was relieved to see me so warm and cheerful. The woman brought me a deep dish of hot soup and ordered me to sit down and eat it.

I fell asleep while eating the soup. I was aware that Wladek took me out of the chair and laid me on the window seat, which he softened with his sheepskin jacket. He covered me with my coat and I slept while he proceeded to warm his bones with innumerable shots of vodka.

I slept but my ears were listening. Was I dreaming? Or was Wladek telling the innkeeper what had brought him to Tarnopol?

"Of course I wouldn't be wandering on this road on foot if it hadn't been a very important matter, you understand?" he said with a tone of self-importance. Sitting squarely with both elbows on the table, in one hand a shot glass, in the other the half-empty bottle of vodka.

"You see," he was saying as he swallowed yet another drink, throwing his head back, "Mr. Spira knows me. He knows I can do anything! That is why he sent me and not Antek, who really wanted to go."

It was at the mention of my uncle's name that I sat up and realized what was going on. Plainly, Wladek was drunk and was in the process of spilling the beans. I jumped off the window seat, and with lightning speed ran to him, grabbing him by the sleeve. I tugged and pulled and pleaded. "Let's go! Uncle, I have to go make pee-pee!"

Not giving him time to think, I pulled as hard as I could until we were outside. I scooped the freshly fallen snow into my cupped hands and threw it into Wladek's face. He shook his head as if to clear it further, and, realizing what had happened, he spoke to me. "Thank you, Miss Yona. My God, what was I doing?"

"None of that 'Miss Yona', you told me we are supposed to be related." I said.

He held his head in his hands, moaning excuses, chastising himself severely for what he realized he had almost told the innkeeper.

Grabbing his elastic suspenders, I said, waving my finger, "No more vodka."

No one paid any attention to us when we returned to the inn. Other peasants were sitting around drinking vodka and complaining about their problems. We were lucky no one was really listening to Wladek when he started recounting his exploits.

In the morning we hitched a ride on a potato wagon. The farmer dropped us near the train station.

We arrived in Slomniki late that evening. My grandparents and my uncle Mooniu were elated to have me with them at last.

Everyone questioned me for hours after I arrived, about everything. Exhausted from the trip and all the talking, I slept a lot during the next few days.

CHAPTER 8

Grandparents

Back to square one! New people, new town, new house . . . everything is new. New feelings. People are behaving like they used to, going about their daily chores. There is no ghetto. Not so many Germans in the streets. Life seems to be more normal.

I feel out of place. The new surroundings take some getting used to.

My grandparents are acting as parents now. They are too old for that, but having me here is obviously a great relief to them. They tell me they don't have to worry about me anymore.

I knew them so well before I left, but I don't know them so well anymore . . . why, I wonder, do they seem so different now? Maybe it isn't them. Maybe it's me! After all, I am older, and so many things have happened since September 1939.

My Babcia (grandmother) is adorable. She's round and just a little taller than me. She dotes on me. From the moment I came she hasn't stopped feeding me. We have plenty to eat, fresh vegetables and fruit and meat every day. It's nothing like it was in the ghetto in Tarnopol.

Uncle Mooniu lives in Krakow. He has special permission to travel and he comes home for weekends. Dziadziu (Grandfather) wants to know everything about the business, so Mooniu tells him everything that goes on in the office.

And Dziadziu has changed his mind about girls—he likes me a lot now. We go for long walks through the town, down the main street, to the coffee house for an aromatic cup of coffee where he and other old men with white beards have heated conversations. I think all of them must have gone to the same tailor. They all dress alike . . . black suit, white shirt, black velvet hat.

My Dziadziu has a black cloth coat lined in brown seal. The collar is black and the fur is very different, long and shiny . . . Dziadziu told me it was monkeys, but I don't believe him! How could anyone kill monkeys and make a collar out of them?!

Babcia has bought me a white *kożuch*. It is a pretty coat made of sheepskin. The fur is on the inside, and with my mittens from Aunt Regina, I am never cold.

Dziadziu thinks I am really something. He is very proud of me now. He thinks out loud when we are together, and he sometimes asks me what I think. We have an agreement—I go with him in the mornings, but after lunch he lets me go tobogganing with the kids. Down the street there is an empty lot with quite a slope, great for sliding.

Our next-door neighbors, the Makowskis, have four children. Marysia is just about my age, Tadziu is older, and the other two boys are younger.

I am so happy since I met Marysia. We play when I am allowed to go to her house. She has the same Shirley Temple doll my father bought for me at the last World's Fair.

One day Uncle Mooniu came home on a Wednesday, in the middle of the afternoon. Usually he was never home before Friday or Saturday. Surprised as I was to see him, I did not think to worry.

Slowly, he took off his hat and coat and hung them on the hook in the entry hall. He entered the sunlit room, and I saw his face. His cheeks were drooping, and under the thick eyeglasses his eyes were red and swollen.

Uncle Mooniu had been crying. He stood there staring at me with a very sad expression, and after a long moment he asked me to go out and play.

I spent the afternoon with my friend Marysia. When I came back it was evening, and I worried that Dziadziu would reprimand me for coming home so late.

I had completely forgotten about Uncle Mooniu. As I opened the door, it struck me that the room was too dark. *Why haven't they turned on the lights?* I wondered.

They were at the table. Babcia, her face covered with both hands, was quietly sobbing. Dziadziu's eyes were closed, tears running down his cheeks; he was praying out loud.

Mooniu looked in my direction. Still no one spoke.

"What's wrong?" I ask. "Why are you crying? What has happened? Please, tell me!"

Mooniu took me in his arms and held me while he sobbed. He said not a word, just held me. So I cried with him. We cried together for a very long time. When our tears dried and there were no more, Mooniu told me everything.

"You know I have been getting news from your parents through Sweden. I always tell you when I send them packages. These packages are sent through the Swedish

Red Cross to Russia by my friend Mr. Weiss, who lives in Stockholm. Today I received a telegram from Mr. Weiss about your parents."

Here he stopped, his voice wavering, swallowing the lump in his throat. "Apparently, when your father received an affidavit from his uncle inviting him to come to America, your parents decided to go to the United States through east Russia and the Bering Sea to Alaska. It is very cold there and somewhere along the way they perished from the cold. This is what the telegram said."

Perished means they died? I close my eyes. I shut my heart and my soul. I want to die. I want to see it all. I conjure up the images. I can hear the Russian voices. I know what they are saying: "Philip Yacubovitch and his wife are dead!"

I can't see their faces, but I can see them lying in the snow. My father wears a gray suit and a gray herringbone overcoat. The coat is lined with fur and has a fur collar. A gray felt hat covers his hair. He looks warm. My mother's fur hat sits tilted on her head. She is also in gray, wearing her broadtail coat and muff. On her feet she has those beautiful dark-gray platform shoes made of lizard and suede.

They both look so peaceful and elegant. I wonder why they were so careless as to let themselves die. They were properly dressed for cold weather, only my mother did not have proper shoes. She has such beautiful legs and she loved to wear high heels.

I am trying to see them for the last time. I know they will be taken away, but I cannot see their faces. I look around and there is nothing, just a flat, endless landscape of white powder. They are gray. Everything else is white. My mother and father are lying on a white bed of down.

I feel fury mounting like a hurricane in my gut. I am so angry, I shout at my father, "How careless of you to die! How careless and inconsiderate! Wasn't it enough that you left me? Did you also have to die?!"

Someone grabs my arms. I look and see Babcia shaking me awake. I am still in the chair. Was I asleep sitting up? I try to shake off that eerie feeling of having just come in from another world. I am ill. My stomach feels like someone left a fist there. I tell Babcia I'm not well. She puts me to bed. Mooniu holds my hand and strokes my hair.

I am back in that state again, where I hear everything faintly. I feel a wave of nausea coming on. My body stiffens. I have rolled myself into a ball. I am shaking . . . inside me there is an earthquake. Thoughts float in and out of my brain. I try to keep the scary ones at bay, not to let them in and invade me. Ha! It's as if I were trying to stay dry in the rain with a paper umbrella.

I know *they* will never come back. I am alone forever. Now I am an orphan.

Dziadziu complains to God. He has been praying, his head completely hidden under his *talles* (prayer shawl). He mutters under his beard in soft monotones and then wails and laments loudly, as if making sure God will hear of his grief. Babcia goes about her business, dabbing her eyes with a handkerchief, which she constantly pulls out and puts back into her sleeve.

I think about God. How come he took my parents and then let them die?

I ask Dziadziu, "What can God really do? Tell me the truth! I must know. I saw such terrible things in the ghetto. I don't think God should have let them happen. And my parents? How could he let them die? Doesn't he know I am small and I need them?"

Dziadziu has to tell me! He realizes this is very important. He would otherwise never allow me to disturb his prayers. He tries to explain to me the depth of his belief and devotion. God is good. We don't always understand his ways. God knows what he is doing.

But I want God to reconsider and give me back my parents. I want them to come for me. I want them back!

Nothing doing. Dziadziu won't commit himself. God may be almighty but he doesn't make promises.

I carry my grief in my stomach. I will not eat. For days, Babcia cooks my favorite dishes but nothing will go down. She coaxes me to drink some Ovaltine . . . two sips, that's all . . . can't drink anymore. I want to please her but the thought of eating makes me gag.

That first week is eternal.

But slowly, daily events intrude on my sadness, and sometimes I forget for a while.

CHAPTER 9

Gaby Is Back.
I Am in Heaven

My grandparents were always very good to me while I lived
with them in Slomniki. But they were old—too old to be
bringing up a child my age.

At the beginning, when I first came from Tarnopol, I
missed the family I left behind. I missed Aunt Regina and
Tushek even more. I adored Tushek. He was my favorite
cousin. He was so funny. He made me laugh all the time.
And even though Kuba and I fought like cats and dogs, we
were close and he had been my playmate. It was with Kuba
that I did the most mischievous deeds. He always managed
to lead us both straight into trouble.

Here in Slomniki I am alone with my grandparents, and
I wait with great impatience for Saturdays when Mooniu
will come from Krakow to spend the weekend with us.
When he comes he brings daily papers—sometimes good
news, sometimes bad—and many other things that are now
to be found only in the big city.

As soon as Uncle Mooniu arrived that day, I knew he
was bringing good news. He was so excited and happy. He
could hardly sit still!

Finally, his son was coming home! He hadn't seen Gaby for a long, long time! At the sound of the doorbell, he ran to open the door.

The boy stood quietly in the open doorway, his eyes filled with tears and his body trembling. Uncle Mooniu extended his arms, but Gaby didn't move. Uncle Mooniu bent down and put his arms around Gaby and gently, very gently, pressed him to his heart. All the rest of us were silent; we just stood and watched and cried until Mooniu has had his fill, and then we took turns hugging and kissing Gaby.

He hadn't changed much; he was still a shy little boy, and although he had grown and was thinner, he was still as beautiful as when we had parted.

He wasn't sure about anybody else in the room, but he knew me instantly. He was as happy to be back with me as I was to have him here. I gave him my bed and I slept on the floor beside him.

As soon as he was willing, with Babcia's permission, I took him to meet the Makowski children. I told Marysia that he was almost my brother. I wanted him to be known as my brother; it was very important to me.

I convinced Gaby to make a pact signed in blood. I remembered a story my cousin Henryk had read to me in Tarnopol about Indians: "To be blood brothers you have to mix your bloods together so you can never again be separated." I told him and he believed me. I pricked my finger with a needle from Babcia's sewing basket. At first the pinprick didn't produce any blood, so I did it again and a round drop of blood appeared on the tip of my finger. Gaby wasn't so sure he wanted to participate in this game, but I forced him.

"We are forever united in blood," I pronounced in a solemn voice. And with my eyes closed, I conjured up all the magic words Tushek had invoked to impress me with his power. Gaby was transfixed. His bloody finger was proof positive that we were blood brothers, and no one could ever separate us again.

Gaby was a wonderful child. He had the sweetest disposition. Babcia and Dziadziu adored him. And I could have been jealous if I didn't love him so much myself.

The Makowski children, Gaby, and I became inseparable. We played together whenever we could. Sometimes Marysia came to our house. Babcia liked her a lot; we played very quietly. The boys were too loud and too active; they played in the street or at the Makowskis. On the other hand, they ate at our house whatever Babcia fed them. We were not allowed to eat at their house—my grandparents were kosher, and Dziadziu worried we might be fed pork.

Marysia and the boys went to school, and came home to eat around one. I sat in the window waiting for her. Soon I would know what she had learned that day. She told me everything.

Marysia wore a uniform, a long-sleeved navy blue smock with two big patch pockets and a round white pique collar. I wanted one just like hers . . . and the briefcase she wore on her back with all the books and pencils and erasers. That too I wanted, to be like her—normal.

Mrs. Makowski fed her children the main meal of the day when they came home from school. They washed their hands, and the whole family ate together. Sometimes I sat and calculated how long she would be eating, and sometimes I couldn't wait—so I ran downstairs and met her on the street.

After lunch everyone did homework. I went to work with Marysia. I read better than she did, but I didn't write as well. We did the arithmetic together. She became the teacher and proudly explained all she had learned that day. We learned to add and subtract together.

One day I said to Babcia, "I wish I could go to school. Why won't you let me?"

"It is impossible," she said "But instead of the navy smock you want so much, I will take you to the dressmaker's and have new dresses made for you."

So I got a new red dress with a white collar and a white dress with multicolored dots and a third dress of white pique with my monogram embroidered right in the center of the chest. I liked pretty clothes, so the dress made me happy—but not like a blue school smock would have!

We have a new passion, Marysia and I. We love to go into the fields and pick wildflowers. Slomniki is a quiet little town surrounded by forests, fields, and pastures. In minutes we are out of town, looking for new specimens that we have never pressed before.

We go early in the morning; days have become too hot. The wheat in the fields has begun to yellow. We skirt the fields for red poppies and blue cornflowers. We are careful not to trample the wheat, as it will not rebound anymore; it is too late in the season.

Yellow buttercups and bluebells grow by the roadside or on the edge of the forest. Little white daisies dot the pastures. We bring home flowers by the armload and then sit quietly and place them between the pages of a very thick and heavy book, carefully arranging their petals and leaves flat so they will dry open and look like they are still alive.

When we are bored with flowers, we run down to the pasture where the cows are. With our butterfly nets we chase butterflies, which we never intend to catch!

We pick berries and hazelnuts in season. We invent tools to help us reach the ripest fruit, or cross a stream, or climb a tree. Sometimes we run until exhausted and plop down in the middle of a patch of those tiny daisies that grow in the pastures, and we weave crowns for our heads and compose fairy tales for our hearts.

I am the princess today, and tomorrow I will be the bad witch; Marysia and I alternate roles. The brothers Grimm and Hans Christian Andersen provided most of the material, but our own imaginations soared out of bounds, and we moved into the future with tall tales of high adventure.

"Someday I will go beyond mountains and oceans to a land where . . . everything is wonderful and peaceful and safe." That part of the tale I believed implicitly; the gypsy had told me about it the day on the hill when she looked at my palms and foretold my future.

It happened just at the beginning of winter. The first snow had piled up enough for Tadziu's toboggan to be taken out of storage. Marysia, Gaby, Tadziu, and all the rest of us trooped up to the top of the hill, waiting for our turns to slide down, when I noticed a strange little boy staring at us from behind a tree. There was a deep frown on his forehead, and his enormous black eyes were full of such wonder, as if he had never seen anything like this before. It was pretty obvious that he too wanted to join our group and slide down the hill on Tadziu's toboggan.

Our playground was an empty lot that ran all the way down to the cholera cemetery, where at the bottom of the hill a double barbed-wire fence separated the two.

Now it was our turn, and Marysia and I would go down together. Marysia was steering. She had priority, since it was her toboggan. I sat behind her waving my arms in the air, showing off, so sure of my expertise in tobogganing—when all of a sudden, on the next sharp turn, I fell off the sled and wound up in the deepest snow—right under the fence!

Marysia was already climbing back, laughing at me, pulling the sled up the steep incline, while I was having great difficulty digging myself out of the snow.

Suddenly I saw the little gypsy boy careening down the hill on our toboggan, coming straight at me—only he was not steering! He didn't know how to steer! He was going to run right into the barbed-wire fence!

"Pull the string to the left!" I screamed.

There was no time to do anything else—I threw myself against the moving sled and bumped the boy off into the fluffy snow.

From the top of the hill where she had been standing, she leapt like a wild animal, and with superhuman strides she flew down, her long skirts billowing like a multicolored balloon. She slid to her knees and embraced her little boy. With her thumbs she cleared away the snow from his eyelids and kissed his face all over.

Then, with a contemptuous growl, she pushed him aside. She stood up and took my hands into hers. Slowly she pulled off my gloves, and in an almost inaudible whisper, her eyes fixed on my palms, she foretold my future: "You will have much pain and suffering, and your life will be endangered!"

Her voice was so low and ominous that I wanted to run, but she held on to my hands and continued: "Don't be afraid of the gypsy," she said, and then looked straight into my eyes. "I will tell you the truth. You need not be worried because like the little doe in the forest, you hear everything, you see everything, and you will know everything you have to know. You will live and grow to be beautiful, in a country far away from here, beyond mountains and oceans, on the other side of the world. Good fortune will smile on you. Now remember what I've told you; you will see it will all come true."

With that she let go of my hands, and bending down, she kissed my forehead and whispered in my ear, "Thank you for saving my son from the barbed-wire fence."

I stood motionless, staring at my palms, completely mesmerized by what had just happened to me. When I looked up, she was gone. Vanished. She disappeared as she had appeared—as if magic had had something to do with it.

Afterward, I no longer wanted to play with the rest of the kids; unmoved by their protests, I went to tell it all to my Babcia.

Every time Marysia and I invented new stories, I remembered the gypsy's words, especially about going to the other side of the world—which I imagined to be quite different from this side, where I was now residing.

Sometimes I saw this other place as a jungle, overgrown with dense and exotic plants, where wild animals were tame and gentle, and people didn't wear any clothes. And sometimes it was just the opposite: castles and green parks and beautiful men and women, elegantly dressed, rich, and totally civilized.

No one had ever told me about the other side of the world. I had no idea where it was, but it was great for making up some of our most fantastic stories.

Altogether, it was a good summer.

CHAPTER 10

"The Action" in Slomniki

Uncle Mooniu came home as much as they allowed him and slept with us on Saturdays and Sundays. When he came from Krakow, he brought us foods that were now impossible to find if you did not have special connections. He brought us coffee and tea and pepper, and my sweet dear babcia always shared some of it with Mrs. Makowski, whose apartment was on the same floor as ours. Mrs. Makowski, in turn, baked cookies with butter that her husband brought home, and she always reminded Babcia that we could eat them because they were made with butter, not lard.

Every week when he came, Uncle Mooniu complained about the changes that were happening in Krakow but, so far, we were not affected by them in this little town where there were not so many Germans and where there was no ghetto.

And then it happened!

"ACHTUNG! ACHTUNG! ALLE JUDEN RAUSS! SCHNELL!"

Oh, my God, what is happening?

Babcia and Mooniu are looking out the window.

I jump out of bed and look out the window with Mooniu. It's still night out there!

Oh my God, what is this?

There are hundreds of people in the middle of the street.

Women and children are being pushed out of their houses by the Gestapo. The children are crying, the women are carrying bundles and suitcases and milk cans. Some men are being beaten with rubber hoses.

Are they going to kill us now?

They kick and shout: *"RAUSS, MACH SCHNELL!"*

Those horrible guttural sounds are getting closer to our building.

Gestapo! I can tell by the way they march. No one else walks like them. They own that sound. It's theirs. They pound their authority right into the pavement with each step. Their black-booted feet have a purpose. They have come here to trample all us Jews into one bloody pulp!

Today is our turn. Slomniki is being made *"YUDEN-REIN."* This is the day for relocation: they have come to clean this peaceful little town of all its Jews . . . the vermin, the subhuman swine who offend their Aryan sensibility. They have to be removed, disposed of, terminated. I don't understand any of it.

Dawn is breaking. Again I look out of the window and now recognize most of the faces. All my dziadziu's friends are there in the middle of the street, being pushed and beaten.

Mooniu says, "Don't be afraid. I have this special document from the commandatur in Krakow. This will protect us. They wouldn't dare override the authority of this signature."

I feel reassured. Uncle Mooniu will protect us. Babcia and Dziadziu are dressed. We are prepared. Gaby is still asleep. I am about to wake him when Babcia says, "Mooniu, take the children to the Makowskis' while there's still time. They will be safe with them."

Uncle Mooniu carries Gaby across the hall to our neighbors and deposits his sleeping son in the middle of the bed, between Tadziu and Janusz, the two Makowski boys.

I come back with my uncle to the apartment.

Babcia is appalled!

"Go back! Stay with Marysia!"

She pushes me out the door. I don't want to leave her!

They are coming up the stairs. The noise of the boots on the stone steps is deafening. Can't go that way anymore. Babcia grabs my hand and pulls me into the kitchen.

"Out the back door! Fast! Go on!"

I won't leave her. Anyway, it's too late now. There are more Gestapo coming up the back stairs. I could have made it before, but I didn't want to leave her. Not again, even to be with good neighbors like the Makowskis. My mother left me with Regina; Regina sent me to Babcia! I don't want to leave Babcia! Oh, no! I will go with her wherever she goes!

As the Gestapo enters the room, we are all respectfully quiet. *"KOMMEN SIE RAUS! ALLE! MACHT SCHNELL!"*

Mooniu smiles and reaches for the framed document that is hanging on the wall. "Herr Commandant, we have this special permission." He hands it to the man with the gloves.

The officer hardly glances at the document and throws it on the floor with disdain. *"RAUS DU SCHWEIN, KEINE EXCEPZION MACH SCHNELL."*

Mooniu pleads, "Herr Commandant, please, I must go back to Krakow. When my boss finds out you have detained me, you might get into trouble."

"You presumptuous dog!" The rubber hose connecting with skin makes a dull clap. Mooniu grabs the side of his face. Blood flows through his fingers. He has a deep gash across his whole cheek.

Babcia runs to him, getting between the Gestapo officer and her son. The commandant hits her on the head and opens the skin on her forehead.

I know this is the end of us!

No one would hit an old woman like Babcia. These men are monsters, not men like any other! They have no feelings—you can see it in the expressions they wear on their faces. There is cruelty and meanness in their eyes. They are hard as steel.

Mooniu takes his mother by the elbow and we go down to the street.

The column of people is swelling by the hundreds as they are being herded into the middle of the street like cattle.

I feel nauseated. It must be fear!

Babcia holds me tight. Dziadziu and Mooniu are swallowed by the crowd and surrounded.

"What do you think is happening?"

"What will they do with us?"

"Do you think they will put us in a ghetto?"

"That is what they are saying."

"Maybe they need some new labor so they will take us to work."

"Yes, that must be it!"

They are all looking for some hope.

"But why the women and children and all the elderly?"

"Herr Spira, you go to Krakow to work, you must know something."

"I know nothing. I will try to find out if I can. But now is not the time."

Some people have bundles. Some have baskets with food and old-fashioned enamel cans filled with milk.

The sun is getting stronger by the minute and the temperature is rising. Today will be a heat wave, like there are sometimes in Poland in the middle of the summer. The air is still, the humidity high. It's heavy and oppressive. Nature has conspired with the Gestapo.

We are being marched to the edge of town. At the end of the main street there is a school. We are enclosed . . . like pigs in a pen. We are waiting to be transported.

The schoolyard is fenced in. The back of the schoolyard is adjacent to the cholera cemetery, like the lot where we went tobogganing. No one is ever allowed to go there. That's why there is barbed wire on that fence.

The Germans have opened the doors to the classrooms and are pushing us into them. I am being suffocated. I can't breathe. Everyone is taller. My face rubs against the dark, rough fabric of their clothing. Dziadziu picks me up into his arms and pushes toward the only window in the room. He wants me to put my head out the window and breathe the outside air.

I feel better, but now there is no space to put me down on the floor. We are squeezed in like sardines. There is not a square centimeter of open space.

Some people have been standing for hours. Tired, they slip to the floor. Everyone is squeezed a little more as they sit down.

We are lucky. We are by the window. At least we can breathe. It is so hot, almost unbearable. Everyone is sweating. The body odors are becoming stronger. A woman in the corner faints. Someone is asking for water or smelling salts.

We are waiting . . . ! But we don't know what we are waiting for.

When they open the door and call all the younger, able-bodied men to come out, we speculate. Why them? What will they do with them?

Mooniu has left the room with the other men. They are given picks and shovels. The fence between the schoolyard and the cholera cemetery is torn down. The men are digging a ditch so long and so wide.

I look out the window and I think we are lost.

We are not the same as we were yesterday.

We are locked up in a small classroom, hundreds of people stuffed into a space where, at most, twenty students would sit.

Ha. What a joke. My wish has come true. I am in school.

My position at the window allows me to see the activities in the yard. All those shovels are digging one enormous hole.

Mooniu stops for a moment. He's on top of the heap of earth. He sees the Gestapo officer in charge coming toward him. He takes something out of his pocket and shows it to him. The Gestapo reads it and then motions for Uncle Mooniu to follow him.

I can't see either of them anymore. Uncle Mooniu doesn't come back to the classroom at night when all the others return. Where is Uncle Mooniu? We speculate that he has been released. Maybe we will be set free also.

This place is unbearable.

There are guards in front of the doors and at the windows. The building has four classrooms, two on each side of a central corridor. At the end of this corridor there is a water faucet with a white enamel bowl underneath.

During the still of the night, through the open transom window, I hear the water dripping. Tic . . . tic . . . tic . . . I can see the drops splashing on the bottom of the bowl. I am thirsty. The last bit of liquid I had was yesterday evening when the woman with the milk can offered Babcia a few sips, trying to divide the little bit she had left among the three of us.

I have never felt so oppressed. But I don't cry anymore, not since my parents died. Tonight is the worst night of my life. I cannot sleep. I am so afraid. I know we are in danger.

Today is as hot as it was yesterday. No cool breezes. No water. No food. Just stench and fear. The men are digging deeper. *What will they put into that hole?* I wonder.

"I would give anything for a drink of water," I hear someone say.

Me too, I think. So I will go and get some water. Not far to go, just to the faucet that drips all night, down at the end of the corridor.

I say nothing but take the white enamel can that is standing empty behind me.

I stand up, and stepping over my babcia, I hoist myself to the windowsill. I swing my legs to the other side and jump off, landing on the gravel beneath the window. I think I mustn't fall or I will scrape my knees.

Crunch, crunch, crunch . . . noisy little pebbles. The guard is looking at me and doesn't say a word. I don't care if he kills me! I am going to get some water.

Down the hallway . . . to the end.

I see the spigot.

Ah! The can smells foul from the soured milk. I rinse it and fill it full of water. The top of the can could be used for drinking. I fill it to the brim and drink until there is not a drop left. I let the water run on my arms. I fill it again and turn around, expecting the two guards at the door to shoot me. No one there. They are outside talking with their comrades.

Quietly, I try to slip by them. They see me. One of them asks me something in German. I do not answer. They laugh. I wonder why they are laughing at me. I am at the window.

Dziadziu's eyes are scared. He grabs the water can and hands it to someone behind him. He picks me up and pulls me into the room.

My heart is pounding like a hammer, and so is Dziadziu's. I can feel it.

He says, "That was very foolish, what you did. You could have gotten killed!"

The old man next to Dziadziu has been given some water. He takes a few sips, and with trembling hands gives back the cup. Then, touching his thumbs together, he spreads his fingers, making a V with each hand. Then, placing them on my head, he pronounces a solemn benediction.

Dziadziu explains, "He asks God to look after you, to never forget you, to bless you, and to keep you so that no harm would come to you ever. Amen."

My dziadziu is very tall and portly; he has great difficulty sitting on the floor. Someone who knows him has offered a suitcase for him to sit on. He places it upright and sits, leaning against the wall. His eyes are closed and his head is bobbing up and down. Every once in a while a faint sound escapes his mouth, and I know he is praying. He is a pious man, and I think he has a direct line to God . . . he talks to him so much.

I don't know why, I think about Marysia. Where is Marysia now? She's getting ready to go to school. The sun has just risen over the horizon; that's when her mother wakes her to get her ready for school. Oh, but not yesterday or today. She can't go to school! I am in her school! Locked up! The same classroom where she has been learning, I am locked up!

Why am I locked up?

No one wants to answer my questions. Still, I keep wondering . . . why? What makes me so different? I know I am a Jew, but what is a Jew? I still can't understand.

I try to imagine what this room looked like when Marysia came here to school. The blackboard is still on the wall opposite the window. So? The pupils sat with their backs to the schoolyard, all the tables lined up in neat rows. I close my eyes and imagine: I hear the bell and I see all the children running out to play in the yard during recess. I hear Marysia reading and Tadziu writing numbers on the big blackboard, adding and subtracting, like all children do when they are in school.

But there is no bell and there are no children . . . only the ones rolled up like anchovies, lying on their parents' bodies, squeezed into crevices, draped over bundles, smelling of urine, vomit, and excrement. Jewish children only.

And this is not a classroom. This is a waiting room. We are all waiting. Some say they don't know what for. But I know! I know!

I know why the hole was dug . . . right in the cemetery.

"Everybody out! Rauss!"

The waiting is over.

I hear shots.

They are lining us up, all the old ones and the children. Useless lot.

Babcia and Dziadziu know we are going to die. Right here, right now. They cry. I don't want to.

I don't want to look back, into the ditch that is right behind me, but I can't help hearing.

They tell me not to be afraid. I don't know what it feels like to die! I saw Bernard the cripple die right in front of my eyes! There was nothing to it.

There are many Gestapo right in front of us, with guns. They are ready to shoot. I cannot look at their faces. I see the black hole at the end of the gun, staring at me like a malevolent eye.

I smell the sweat of fear. I hear the flies in the pit behind me.

"Spira, David!"

"Spira, Salomea, and a child!"

"Here! Here! I am David Spira and here is Salomea." Arms held high, he shouts.

"*Komen sie mit.*"

We step out of the line.

We are led out of the schoolyard and loaded onto a truck full of able-bodied men and women. We are the only family in the truck. I don't know why. The rest have been separated from theirs.

Sylvia, a young woman who is my Babcia's dressmaker, inches her way over and asks Dziadziu, "Do you know where they are taking us now?"

He has no idea. He doesn't even know why the commandant pulled us out of that line, where we stood waiting to fall into the ditch. The only two old people, and me, the only child. Dziadziu believes God certainly had something to do with it.

It is a long and shaky ride . . . once again we are stuffed in like sardines. Someone vomits. Now I know that people vomit and even become incontinent when they are terribly afraid. I feel nauseous all the time.

We are unloaded in a place surrounded by barbed wire. When all the trucks are emptied, they march us to the barracks. There are several other children. All seem older than I am. There are some elderly people. I am with Babcia. Dziadziu went with the men.

The next day we are told we are going to work while we are waiting to be resettled. Sylvia says I should go to work with her. She takes me under her wing. She ties a kerchief on my head to make me look older. I do everything she tells me to do. We have to stay alive so Mooniu can find us. I believe he will save us like he did before.

In the next few days we get a message from Mooniu. A man, who comes to this place with a truck to deliver something, brings a letter. Mooniu has a connection with someone very high up, the same person who got him out of the action in Slomniki.

In the meantime, I behave like the rest of the women, who are twenty or thirty or older. I work in the kitchen. I peel potatoes. I can handle small and medium potatoes without any trouble. My hands have become very agile. Today I've peeled so many the women are starting to count, just for fun. As fast as I can, I peel, like a machine. I reach into the basket and dig for the small potatoes . . .

Suddenly my hand is pinned by a knife! The knife is sticking in my hand! I follow it up the blade to the handle, to the hand that is holding it . . . white skin covered with freckles and pale blond hair, green sleeve . . . uniform!

Slowly I lift my head and look him straight in the eye. For a second our eyes are locked. Then he smiles. The smile is twisted, like a grimace. He pulls out the knife and bursts out laughing. A loud, gurgling laugh, as if he had staged a very funny comedy.

His boyish face, with rosy cheeks, is belied by the cruelty in his baby-blue eyes, and his laughter sends a chill down my spine.

As soon as he is gone, a woman whose name I cannot remember tears her handkerchief into strips. They wash the wound and bandage my hand to stop the bleeding. And I don't cry. The cut is in the fleshy part of my palm. They bandage it tight so it doesn't hurt me now, not even a bit, not now, not later. I won't feel it; that's all.

Later in the barracks I show Babcia my wound. She cries and cries. She's terribly afraid in this place.

Some time passes. I don't know how long. Mooniu sends a message. Dziadziu is out. Tomorrow he will send a man with papers, a special paper to get Babcia and me.

The papers must be good. No questions, no problems.

The ride back to Krakow is not very long. We arrive at dusk. When Mooniu sees us in the dim light of the warehouse, he bursts through the door and comes to us, running. His short, stocky frame is somehow reduced . . . . He looks tormented, haggard, and abused. On one side of his face there is a gauze bandage. The cheek is very swollen, the cut infected. The swelling imbalances his face. He looks like some grotesque rendition of himself. Poor dear Uncle Mooniu, such a devoted, loving son must have died a thousand deaths from the time he left Slomniki . . . until just now, this very moment.

He grabs Babcia and encircles her with his arms. His whole body shakes as he weeps. They stand bound together, sobbing, releasing the terror and pain and fear pent up inside them, and for a brief moment they look like they are one.

Slowly Babcia disengages from Mooniu's embrace. She strokes his head and whispers, "Sha! Sha! Sha!" Her eyes search the room. "Mooniu, where is David?"

"Don't worry, he's fine, and waiting for you at home."

"Where is home?" she asks.

"My home in the ghetto."

CHAPTER 11

Ghetto Number Two

The woman stood politely, silent in the corner of the room, by Mooniu's desk. She waited to be introduced. She looked at both of us in turn, as if to determine something important she had to know about each one separately.

"This is Marta, my secretary." Mooniu turned to his mother and then to Marta, who stepped forward and shyly extended her hand. Babcia took it and held it in both hands for a second, and then her eyes wrinkled into a smile and she warmly acknowledged the introduction. Did Babcia know about Marta?

There was something strange about this moment. Babcia was saying something without any words, and Marta knew that it was important. She was a pretty woman—small, slim, and very shapely. The most arresting features of her otherwise ordinary face were her absolutely enormous blue eyes, which were ever so slightly bulging out of their sockets. Her hair was dark, here and there peppered with gray, and she wore it almost the same way as Aunt Frania, with the two sides rolled up above each ear.

Once in a while Mooniu glanced at Marta. There was an air of conspiracy between them.

As she moved about the room I noticed her shoes. They were high, cork platform wedges and she maneuvered in them like a ballerina. I liked her instantly and decided right there I wanted her to be my friend.

Later, in the ghetto, it is clear we have dislodged her. Mooniu's apartment is small, but quite obviously has had the hand of a woman in it. Yellowed lace curtains on the windows, a beautiful crocheted tablecloth on the dining room table, and a well-equipped kitchen are signs of a woman's presence.

Marta is Mooniu's lover, it's their secret. Marta lives on the floor below us, with a family who sublet her a room.

I am sure Marta is in love with Mooniu; and I am in love with Marta.

Babcia is old and gray, with soft mushy skin, a round tummy, and a soothing, familiar scent. Marta is young and vibrant, and she wears an exotic perfume. Her presence injects a spirit of life into our dreary, frightening existence. She has a record player and she loves music. Sometimes I listen. Sometimes I even dance in her room. She allows me to do many things I cannot do with Babcia. She spoils me.

I think Mooniu loves her also, although I have never seen him say anything directly that was endearing or intimate.

Both of them have special permission to leave the ghetto daily, to go to work at Hartwig's warehouse. Every day I sit by the window and watch them go, praying they will come back that evening. Some people go out and never come back.

Babcia, Dziadziu, and I stay home. Mooniu decided not to bring Gaby into the ghetto. Babcia cooks and I help. Dziadziu sits, silent and morose. For the midday meal I set the table and help Babcia serve. Dziadziu prays before we eat. That's all he does now. All day long, he prays.

In the evening, when Marta and Mooniu come home, there is conversation at the table. I like that so much better than the heavy silence. We all wait for the news they bring from the outside. Times are getting worse.

Today, Mooniu has something very important to tell us. It is a secret, so no one must know. We are sworn to secrecy.

Mooniu wants us to leave the ghetto and live on the outside, on Aryan papers. There is a way to buy false papers if you have the right kind of money, and he has gold dollars.

Dziadziu doesn't want to go anywhere, but Babcia agrees with Mooniu. We should try to get out of the ghetto.

Early this morning, Mooniu went to work. Babcia was busy in the kitchen and I was helping, when all of a sudden she grabbed her chest and swayed. I ran to her.

"Babcia, what is the matter?"

"Give me a chair," she whispered.

I pulled one under her and she sat down, breathing heavily. She was pale as a sheet and I was very scared. I called Dziadziu from the bedroom and as soon as he saw her he said it was her heart. He went quickly to fetch her medicine and then back to the kitchen. Almost in panic, while lifting the dark blue bottle to the light, he moaned, "There are no more drops in this bottle. She needs Valerianna! Do you know where the pharmacy is?"

I nodded. He handed me the bottle, and reaching in his pocket for some money, he said, "Run! As fast as you can!"

I swing down the staircase, four steps at a time. I burst into the street, running. I run all the way to the pharmacy. I see the old green storefront. The word APTEKA and a little cross in a circle are painted red on the windows. I am so winded I can hardly push the heavy glass door open. Mr. Greenberg, the old pharmacist, comes from behind the counter to help me. There is no one inside.

"I don't have any medicines, you know," he says more to himself than to me. "What do you need?"

"Valerianna! It's for my babcia. She must have it. Please! Do you have any?"

Without another word, he takes the little blue bottle from my hand and removes the glass stopper, brings the bottle to his nose and, nodding, disappears in the back.

A moment later, holding both bottles to the light, he proceeds to fill Babcia's prescription.

All of a sudden his eyes are distracted and the steady stream of liquid wavers misses the bottle, and drops fall on the counter. Mr. Greenberg looks terrified.

I turn to see what has so perturbed him. Trucks! Soldiers! Guns! A cold shiver runs through me again. Looks like another action. I must do something not to get caught. I grab the bottle of Valerianna drops.

"Mr. Greenberg, is there any way I can get out of here other than the front door?"

"Come, I will take you to the courtyard. From there you can get out to the side street."

Cautiously I step into the street. Enormous trees form a canopy. The sky is invisible. The shadows will protect me. I run again!

I hear strident, vicious, guttural sounds, the same as in Slomniki: "*ACHTUNG! SCHNELL! RAUSS!*"

Stop! Be careful, I say to myself. I flatten my back against the large tree. The sounds are getting closer.

I see an open portal just a few steps ahead. I jump over the threshold into the black hole. I crouch and squeeze my body into the darkest corner. Footsteps! Is it just one, or are there many? One-two, one-two, one-two. Oh! Oh! No breathing now. An enormous body in the doorway stops the flow of light.

I can see him. He hasn't seen me yet. He comes from the light; his eyes open wide in the dark. He searches. I press my body harder against the cold stone wall, hoping it will absorb me. My head starts spinning. I have to let out the breath I have been holding and take another one or I will faint.

He steps inside and there is some light again. He can see better now. He notices me in the corner. Grabbing my elbow, he forces me to stand. "Come." His command is firm but not brutal.

I start crying. "I must take this to my grandmother. She is ill! Please let me go!" I plead. I show him the little bottle I've been squeezing so hard in my hand.

For a moment he hesitates, and then his grip on my upper arm tightens and he pushes me out the door.

He is young. He looks like he could be swayed. I plead again, this time in German. "*BITTE LASSEN SIE MICH GEHEN.*"

He pushes me out into the street and then turns away and leaves me. He walks toward the crowd waiting in the square to be loaded onto the trucks.

After the roundup there is hysteria in the ghetto. Mooniu decides we are definitely going out on Aryan papers—Gaby and me together, as brother and sister.

Gaby is still in Slomniki; the Makowskis are bringing him to Krakow.

Mooniu says he will get us children out first, and then Dziadziu and Babcia, and then he will go with Marta.

For the moment he feels safe with his special papers. Working at Hartwig he still can leave the ghetto every morning.

His dear friend Professor Michalkiewicz is arranging everything for us. He has found a family who will take us; we will be their relatives from another town.

Now everything is happening very fast. Rumors have it there might be another action soon.

Mooniu and I will leave the ghetto tonight. Who knows what can happen tomorrow?

Babcia has prepared some of my clothes. Marta packs them into a small suitcase. My departure is sudden and very traumatic. The good-byes are wrenching and painful.

Dziadziu makes me promise I will take good care of Gaby, his only grandson, to carry on the family name. He also tells me never to eat pork. There are many other instructions. I promise him everything.

Tonight we sleep in Mooniu's office. Tomorrow, when Gaby gets here from Slomniki, he will make a special place for us to sleep in the warehouse.

We will be in hiding until the papers are ready. Getting good papers made takes a long time.

"I don't know yet what your names will be, but you will go as sister and brother, and you will have baptismal certificates, which are the best proof that you are not Jews. Also a whole new family history. There is only one thing you will have to be very careful about—that is, that no one should ever see Gaby's genitals."

"Genitals? What are genitals?"

"His pee-pee." Uncle Mooniu patiently tries to explain about circumcision. He uses big words that I try to understand. All this embarrasses him; I can tell by his voice.

"There is a skin that covers a little boy's penis. When he is a week old, all Jewish boys are circumcised, which means that this piece of skin is cut away." I gasp at the thought. Mooniu reassures me. "Don't worry, it doesn't hurt. Therefore, if you see a Jewish boy and a Gentile boy naked, their penises will look different. One has a skin covering its tip and the other one doesn't.

"If the Germans suspect that your papers are false, they make you drop your pants to see if you are circumcised. And then they know for sure.

"You must never allow Gaby to pee in front of anybody. No one must ever see that he is circumcised. There are people everywhere who could denounce you to the Germans. Now you see how important this is? You will have to watch him until he knows not to pee or undress in front of anyone."

Ah . . . finally, I understand! There is a difference! Of course, I could never see it before, could not understand what it was that made Jews, Jews! Now I know! It's a piece of penis skin! But I don't have a penis! What about me? How am I different?

"*You* are not! You are the same as any other little girl you know, the same as Marysia, who is not Jewish."

"I am? And no one can tell that I am a Jew?"

"That's right! And with blonde hair and blue eyes, no one will ever suspect you."

All of this is very confusing. Gaby is different than other boys, but I am not. So . . . there is an advantage, after all, to being a girl. I wonder if Dziadziu would agree.

Ever since that day when the Germans entered Zloczow and shot Bernard the cripple, right in front of me, without reason, without motive, I have wanted to know: What did we do, we Jews, that they want to kill us all?

Gaby comes and we are both deliriously happy to be together again. Now I am very curious about those other penises, with the skin still attached. What do they look like? How great to have a foreskin and be above suspicion. No chance to be mistaken for a Jew.

CHAPTER 12

We Are Hiding
in the Warehouse

My family is in the clover seed business. They have been Hartwig's tenants for generations. Now Gaby and I explore and play hide and seek in this enormous warehouse. There is one place where the sacks of clover are so big we burrow our bodies into the tiny pungent seed until nothing but our heads are visible. We have done this twice, to hide from unexpected visitors. It took hours afterward to rid myself of the tiny seeds that found their way into every orifice of my body, even into the seams of my clothing.

We wait . . . and wait . . . the days are filled with boredom and fear. We have run out of things to do, to make ourselves feel better.

I miss Babcia and Dziadziu. I ask Mooniu if I can see them. He is appalled!

"Of course you can't! No one must see you or suspect that you are hiding here!"

I have a bad feeling. I don't know if Babcia and Dziadziu are still alive. I think Mooniu is hiding something.

Nobody goes out anymore. We all sleep here at Hartwig's.

I know it is summer now. Every day it gets hotter and hotter in this warehouse. Some days are almost unbearable.

Our food is brought to us in neatly stacked white enamel containers, and the opening of each pot has become the great excitement of the day. Meat must not be available since we haven't had any for days, but summer abounds with delicious fruit and berries, which—made into *pierogi* or *knedle* or cold soups—are my favorite foods anyway.

Nowhere to go . . . nothing to do. The waiting has put everyone on edge. Today I was careless. When the little bell attached to the front door announces someone, we must scurry and hide. Today I took my time, and I whispered a bit too loud. For that Uncle Mooniu reprimanded me sharply. I knew I had done wrong and I felt very guilty. I hid in the back, where the sacks of clover were low and the dark corner cooler. I lay there for hours, my arms crossed under my head, looking up at the ceiling and guessing what my new name will be.

How do you change names? Will I remember who I really am? When I'm called will I respond? What if I forget and give myself away? Maybe I won't like it, this new name, what then? If it is Jadwiga I will hate it, I know. But I know I have no choice. Whatever the baptismal certificate says, that will be it.

I haven't allowed myself to think about parting. That feeling, I already know, is unbearable. I leave it for later. This time there won't be an aunt Regina, or an uncle Mooniu, nor Babcia or Dziadziu. This time just strangers. Not even a friend of the family. I try to convince myself it will be an adventure.

Professor Michalkiewicz comes . . . and I know we are leaving.

Today is the day. Now is the time! Suddenly, I wish it was yesterday, or even a week ago.

The professor, a very close friend of my uncle's, has arranged everything. He and Mooniu examine the papers together, and whisper nodding in agreement—the papers are good, very good!

"Don't worry," I hear him say to Mooniu. "They will be fine. I know Kluszewski, he was a colleague of mine. Good family. The children will be safe."

And now it is time to go! I want to say something but my throat wants to swallow, that's all it wants to do. I can't stop myself. There is nothing in my mouth, not even saliva, and my throat keeps on swallowing. I feel like crying. But I will not! Not now, not today, maybe later when no one can see.

The train leaves shortly, we must hurry! Gaby is happy we are going to the country. He hugs and kisses his father. Curtains of water cover my eyes and I must blindly hold on to the balustrade going down the stairs.

The sunlight in the street is so harsh I cannot keep my eyes open. I blink and wipe away the tears. I am not crying. I pretend it is the sun in my eyes, too much light after the dark warehouse.

We walk to the corner and hop on the tram. A few minutes' ride and we are at the station.

Michalkiewicz carries the suitcase. The train to Katowice is on Platform 4. The smell of steam and trains reminds me of trips I took with my parents before the war . . . to Rabka and Krynica, summer resorts. Countryside vacations! Wonderful times! The memory makes me feel better. I start to feel gay; this will be like going on vacation to the country. My name will be different, but so what? I have had other names. Like the time I played Gretel in *Hansel and Gretel*. I have been in plays many times, and I have had many names and I have been many different people. So now I will be . . .

"Professor Michalkiewicz, what is my name?"

"Your name is Yanka Lesiak!" He tells us to call him "Professor M."

Yanka Lesiak, not bad! I am so glad it's not Jadwiga. I hate that name. Yanka is almost like Yona—easy to remember.

We settle into our compartment. I look out the window and notice how many Gestapo and other German soldiers there are on the platform . . . and I am glad we are leaving.

Professor M. closes the door to the compartment, waiting to make sure we are the only people in it, and in a quiet, reassuring voice starts to teach us our new background. "You are sister and brother. Your given names are Yanina and Gabriel. Your family name is Lesiak. Your father's name was Jan, and your mother's, Aniela. You were born in Lwow.

"One day your parents went to work and never came home again. The neighbors told you they were killed in a bombing. Your parish priest found your mother's only relative, Professor Kluszewski, who lives in Klecza. So that is why you are here. Can you remember that?"

Of course! I repeat the story to him, almost word for word. He is pleased.

"You learn fast. That's good."

He continues with more details: birthdates, names of friends and neighbors. "Your father was a lawyer, your mother a dance teacher. That is why you have been to dance school. Your parents were well-to-do, so you have pretty clothes from before the war. A little too small for you now.

"One thing you must never forget—you don't speak or understand German! I want you to remember this at all times because I know your parents spoke German at home and you had an Austrian governess. Speaking German is a dead giveaway that you are a Jew. Most Jews speak German or Yiddish. You do not! You don't understand a word.

"As of this minute, you are Yanina Lesiak, a Catholic, from Lwow, whose parents disappeared or died in a bombing. Gaby, you are her brother. You have been sent to live with the only family your priest knew about."

He drilled us for the duration of the trip, and when we finally arrived in Klecza I was Yanka Lesiak, with all the details.

Professor M was very impressed with our learning ability. He reminded me one last time about not letting Gaby bare his penis in front of anyone and that now I must never reveal I understand German.

"This train stops here only a minute," shouted the train master. "All aboard!"

CHAPTER 13

I am "Yanka Lesiak" Now

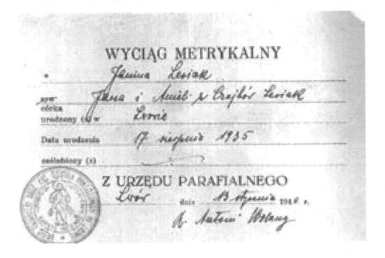

The carriage stood waiting. It was black and shiny. The well-worn, tufted leather seat and the gold lanterns on each side implied old elegance. The horse hitched to the carriage was a beautiful chestnut mare with four white socks and a white star on her forehead.

As the last of the train wiggled out of the station there was no one left on the platform but the three of us. Professor M. waved, and the driver jumped down from the carriage and rushed over in our direction, his hand outstretched to relieve him of the heavy suitcase.

"How are you, sir?" asked the driver.

"Fine, fine, thank you," replied Professor M.

"The professor sent me to pick you up. He's waiting for you at home. Pani Ala and the daughters have gone to church. Such a hot day, isn't it, sir?" said the man as he wiped his face with a handkerchief.

"Leshek, tell me, how is Pan Professor? How are his legs? Is he walking any better?"

"Well, sir, some days he's better than others. When he's strong he can walk pretty fast with the canes. But when he doesn't feel too well his arms are weak and he can't use the canes."

The driver, whom Professor M. had addressed as Leshek, helped Gaby and me into the carriage and we left the station.

The conversation between the professor and Leshek left me very uncomfortable and frightened. What did he mean about his legs? Is the man a cripple?

As if reading my mind, Professor M turned to me and discreetly explained, "Professor Kluszewski has had an illness that left his legs paralyzed. He has to wear special shoes with steel braces, which support his legs, and has to use a cane in each hand to be able to walk."

Gaby was not listening. He sat, shy and quiet, by my side. I held his hand, thinking about this new home and this new family, this man who walks with canes. And, once again, I was frightened.

We are traversing a magnificent landscape. There are patches of gold and dark green and purple and white—colors like I have never seen before—and my eyes distract me from my thoughts. To the right there is a deeply green pasture sloping toward the forest. Cows graze in the shade. Gaby watches with delight. He notices some goats among the cows and jumps up.

"Look!" he shouts. "Look, Yona, a white goat and a black one too!"

I squeeze his hand sharply and pull him down to sit beside me. He looks at me, puzzled, almost in tears. "My name is Yanka," I whisper through my teeth. "Don't forget. From now on we are Gabriel and Yanina Lesiak." Then, with a smile, I repeat, "Two little white goats and a black one! Look, look!"

Leshek turns around. And with a broad smile he says to me, "Wait till you see all the animals. You city children will have such a good time."

Slowly, I realize that this is not a little farm. As we approach a gate, I notice that the fence on each side of it runs completely out of sight.

"We are now in the west garden," says Leshek. "This is the apple and pear orchard. Pan Professor grafts his own trees. This garden used to be his hobby. Now it has become his work."

The horse has slowed to an easy walk. I can hear the flies buzzing. The road is quiet and very dusty, and my white shoes and socks are brown now. I am terribly upset to have become so dirty. What will they think of me, this new family of mine?

Marta told me to put on my white dress with the little black dots. Gaby is wearing short gray pants, which are buttoned all around to a white, short-sleeved shirt. We are both wearing white gloves, and we look very well bred.

Through another gate we enter the courtyard. In the middle there is a well, flanked by four gigantic linden trees.

Facing the big house are the stables, and to the left an enormous barn.

This is my new home. An alien house, full of strangers.

And I, a stranger to myself. Yanka Lesiak now, a child someone else invented.

As I stand, waiting, my throat tightening up again. I have a terrible urge to cry. I don't know why this is happening. I will myself not to—swallowing over and over again till this feeling goes away.

I am Yanka Lesiak. Tomorrow may be different, but this is the day I will remember, hot and brilliant and sunny, the beginning of a new me! I have no reason to cry.

Suddenly I realize Leshek has been talking to me, and until this moment I heard nothing.

He is saying, ". . . Ah? You are wondering about the mill over there?"

"The mill? Oh? Is that what that is?"

"Yes. We make our own flour. The stones are inside the barn. Come, I will show you!"

I am about to follow Leshek when I hear behind me the strangest of noises.

Click!—Click!—Thump—thump—click—click—thump—thump!—

One cane, and then another, appear from the shadows!

The torso of a man bent forward, balancing on the canes. He brings his legs forward one at a time with a jerking motion. He moves slowly. The rubber-tipped canes and the irons on his legs make a strange staccato noise on the wooden planks of the porch.

As he approaches the stairs leading to the courtyard, Michalkiewicz rushes to embrace him. They hold each other for a long moment.

"My dear friend! How are you?"

"I am walking! Some days are better than others. And you? How are things in the big city?"

"Well, I will tell you all about that in a moment. First, let me introduce you to the children." Professor M. looks in my direction and beckons me over. "Yanka, come meet Professor Kluszewski. Where is Gabriel?"

Only now do I notice that the horse and buggy in which we arrived from the station has been led to the stables, with Gaby still in it. I dart across the courtyard, running through the chickens and ducks and geese, which scatter, cackling loudly. A white, bushy dog barks and bares his fangs! I stop abruptly, a few paces from the dog, my heart pounding. Leshek helps Gaby out of the carriage. He runs to me, crying.

Oh, my God! I almost forgot him! I've been told to look after him. How could I be so careless? In the future I will never let him out of my sight. I make this promise to myself as I wipe away his tears.

Professor Kluszewski is waiting for us to be presented. Professor M. makes the introductions. At first I am reticent to come forward, but Professor Kluszewski extends his hand with a smile, and I advance toward him. He shakes my hand and then addresses Gaby, "I'm so glad you are here, we need some more men in this family."

Gaby stands by me, eyes downcast, pushing his chin into his chest. This is not going to be easy for him. After a long and silent moment, he answers politely, "How do you do?" Then, turning to me, his eyes pleading, he asks in an inaudible whisper if we are allowed to go to the stables and look at all the animals.

"You may go, of course, but be careful and don't make your clothes dirty."

This is turning out to be a fascinating place. Imagine, a mill where you make your own flour. Cows who give you milk every day and a garden full of fruit! At least we won't go hungry. That's what Uncle Mooniu said as he was bidding us good-bye, "On a farm there is always something to eat; you will not have to worry about food as we have to worry here in the ghetto."

I think about Uncle Mooniu. As we were parting this morning he whispered in my ear, "Gaby is your responsibility now. Take good care of my son."

CHAPTER 14

Learning to Work
on the Farm

We have decided this is the way we are going to sleep from now on: Gaby at the foot and me at the head of this ancestral bed. Gaby wants to face the wall; he does not want to see out the window at night. The bed is big but not wide enough for us to sleep side by side. The rest of the furniture is dark and overwhelming. The armoire where we have stored our clothing is all carved and full of scary figures. The single door is so heavy I can hardly open it by myself. There is a carved chair in the room. We put our clothes on it when we undress. We do everything together now. I don't let Gaby out of my sight for an instant.

The daughters laugh at us, and they ask if we are afraid to be alone; they think we are afraid of everything. Maybe they are right. I wouldn't want to admit it, but it is probably true. The first few nights in this room were terrible, and we couldn't sleep a wink. The bed was high and plump looking. The sheets were white and stiff. Even though the linen was thick, we felt all kinds of pricks and bites and we were absolutely sure the bed was filled with strange and dangerous creatures that were going to eat us alive if we let ourselves go to sleep. We stayed awake all night, huddled together, and waited for dawn.

Then one morning, as I was being taught to make the bed, I realized the mattress had been recently filled with fresh straw, and the sharp ends were poking through the sheets. It was the straw and not any strange insects that were pricking our tender behinds.

Days run into weeks, and we are getting to know everyone who lives with us on the farm. I like Pan Professor very much, even though he intimidates me, but I don't like Pani Alicia. She has not been very nice to us so far. She is very strict and demanding, and I am really afraid of her.

Katarzyna, whom we call Kasia, is the oldest of the three daughters and definitely the nicest. She is about twenty years old. Her hair and eyes are dark brown, her mouth is thin, but she has a beautiful nose, which gives her face a somewhat aristocratic appearance.

Halina, the youngest, is in her early teens. She's very plain. She appears to be unhappy about Gaby, who is *the* boy in this house. There were no boys here before and she liked it that way.

The middle daughter, Magda, is the beauty in the family. Her perfectly oval face is adorned by a thick mane of curly light-brown hair that she braids and wraps around her head like a crown. She is very different from the other two girls. She's smart, funny, and volatile. She gets angry at the drop of a hat, and when she is really mad her eyes turn dark green and her nostrils flare. She rides horses better than anyone who works on the farm and is as extravagant with her affection as she is with her wrath.

From the very first day she took Gaby under her wing. By now she absolutely adores him. She takes him with her wherever she goes, and I am jealous! But I like her very much, and I make a big effort so she will like me also.

Pani Alicia is not very happy about those two Jewish children who have come to live in her house. Three daughters were enough. She complains, "I don't want any more children to bring up."

The decision to take us in must have been made against her will. She visibly dislikes us, treats me with contempt, and completely ignores Gaby. She's not our favorite, either. No one likes her very much and everyone is afraid of her.

Then, one evening I surprise her at the grand piano in the salon. She plays by candlelight. Her long fingers run on the keyboard as if they had wings. Her whole body moves to the rhythm of the music, and she is a completely different person than the one I know. Her eyes are closed, her face has become soft, and she is smiling while she plays. All at once I know that music is her love. I am in awe. I want to play the piano just like she does.

Every day I learn about something. At first I explore the gardens. Strawberry plants laden with red, ripe berries dangle from the sides of the furrows that line the west garden under the fruit trees. Fascinated by the abundance, I wander through the narrow ditches, one foot in front of the other, crouching every few steps to pick and eat the pungent, sweet strawberries.

There are three gardens, one on each side of the house, at the back is the courtyard. The west garden is the orchard, and all the trees are fruit-bearing.

The cherry season is almost finished. Here and there a few cherries, hidden from birds and inaccessible, still hang on the high branches. There are many varieties. Some are dark red and so sweet they taste like candy. Some are white, with a touch of pink. Those are hard and best used for canning. The sour cherries are still to be picked. Those, I learn later, we will use for baking and cooking and making cherry preserves.

There are raspberry bushes, and gooseberry bushes, and red currant bushes. There are peaches and apricots and plums—at least five different varieties. Most of the apples and pears are winter fruit, and we will leave them on the trees until they ripen and change color, and then we will store them in the cellar for the long, cold winter.

Pan Professor has taken me under his wing. He wants me to follow him wherever he goes. He never tells me where, we just go until we get there.

Now all the girls are absolutely crazy about Gaby. Kasia treats him as if he was her child, and Halina as her baby brother. I don't have to worry about him at the moment.

Pani Ala wants me to help Sofia in the kitchen, but Pan Professor won't let her have me. They fight about it.

Pan Professor says, "I need her with me; she helps me with the grafting, which has been neglected all over the orchard."

I follow him, patiently carrying the tools, the binder, and the saw. I have learned to use the curved knife, and I cut the branches for grafting. I listen and look and learn. I try very hard to please Pan Professor. I want him to like me.

One day Pan Professor tells me that in the fall we are going to start our schooling. Kasia will teach us to read and write, and Pani Ala will give us piano lessons.

"That is what your uncle Maurycy wanted. That was to be part of the arrangement."

At the mention of my uncle Mooniu's name I am instantly taken back to my old self, and a weird feeling overtakes me.

Could it be that I have already forgotten who I really am and have become Yanka Lesiak? Or have I simply forgotten Mooniu and Babcia and Dziadziu on purpose? I haven't thought about them for weeks, maybe months. I don't think that is normal, and I feel ashamed!

Pan Professor notices and wants to know what is wrong with me. I don't know what to say. I am afraid I might say the wrong thing and he will get angry.

But I have become very upset. I want to know where Uncle Mooniu is. Why haven't we heard from him? If he is in touch with Pan Professor, why not with us?

"When did you hear from my uncle?" I ask.

"He sent me the money for your lessons."

"What lessons?"

"The lessons I was telling you about a moment ago. You do understand why you can't go to school?"

I want to know more about Mooniu.

With a sharp word, he cuts off my questions. "You know we must not talk about Uncle Mooniu. You have no relatives, remember?"

We go back to grafting. We work in silence the rest of the day.

Once again fall has painted the rolling hills around us with the most incredible colors. The thick, dark-green pine forests are the only patches that have remained the same. The green of all the grains has turned to yellow. Oats have been cut first, then rye, and now the wheat. The red poppies and blue bachelor buttons are no longer visible anywhere—only the golden shimmer of the ripe wheat undulating in the wind.

On the day the harvest begins, many men come to cut the wheat, and each has a woman who works right behind him. The first man stands at the very tip of the corner of the field, makes the sign of the cross, and begins to cut. His scythe swooshes through the air, and the golden wheat falls to the ground with a moan. He moves rhythmically: one step, one swoosh. When he has cut about three steps, the woman behind him begins to pick up the shafts of the fallen wheat and binds them into a bundle. As she clears the first few steps, the second man begins to cut, with his woman behind him, and so on and so on, until you can see a string of men and women, working in unison with perfect timing. As the first man finishes cutting the first lane, the last one begins.

When the sun is at its peak and the day it's hottest, they all come to eat and rest in the courtyard under the shady trees.

The field that is being cut first is the closest to the house. Maybe wheat ripens there first, or maybe it's tradition. For all the years that I spent on the farm, it was always here that the harvest began.

In the afternoon, when the men take time out to have a smoke, Pan Professor arrives in the courtyard. Some of the women come up to him with their heads bent, and they kiss his hand, and so do some of the men—as they will Sunday in church when they go to greet the priest. Hardly anyone talks.

Pan Professor is the local "lord," and most of the peasants are completely in awe of him. They adore him but are afraid of him at the same time. This may be the reason why he was not afraid to take us in in the first place. He was sure no one would ever dare question him about us, even if they were suspicious.

During the harvest many strangers come in and out of the courtyard. Most look at us without any particular interest. They have seen us in church on Sunday; now they see us work as hard as the rest of the family.

But Farmer Piotr is curious and sly. He wants to know who we are and where exactly we came from. I give him my well-rehearsed story, about my parents and how they were related to Professor Kluszewski. But I worry and wonder why Farmer Piotr is so curious.

Gaby is maturing and he knows what he is not supposed to do. I warn him against strangers who ask too many questions: "Don't say anything, or say you don't remember!"

Maybe Farmer Piotr is nervous because more Germans have come into the village. It has made everyone cautious.

There are checkpoints on the road to Wadowice. Pani Ala was stopped and interrogated. The Germans made her and Magda get out of the carriage while they searched it, asking where she had hidden the money. "What money? I have no money!" she told them. Magda was very brave. She stood defiant, pretending she didn't understand anything.

Pani Ala came home, furious, and took it out on us. "If it weren't for these damn children," she mumbled, "my life could be peaceful. Maybe someone thinks we are getting paid for doing something that's against the law!" she said, and she looked straight at me.

Luckily, the last few months of the year there is so much work I have no time to think, no time to be afraid.

I try to put Farmer Piotr and Pani Ala right out of my mind.

CHAPTER 15

Sunday, My Favorite Day of the Week

Shortly after we arrived in Klecza we were taken to church on Sunday. Most of the time it was the midday Mass that the family attended. I had never been inside a church. The coldness, the awesome light and images of the crucifixion intimidated me at first, but by fall, I was addicted. I loved going to church.

The weather had been unpredictable and I was told to wear a sweater—the white sweater, to go over the red, pleated dress with the white pique collar.

Since Pani Ala was not going with us, we could walk to church. That was also part of the Sunday ritual—meeting and greeting people on the way. After Mass, in front of the church, everyone socializes a little before they disperse and head home.

Today we left home early. The sun was shining brightly, warming the air, and dissipating the morning dampness. Everyone looked spruced up and elegant. Magda was wearing her new flowered dress that Pani Ala brought from Wadowice. It hugged her body at the waist and delineated her round, bouncy behind. Her hair was freed from the tightly plaited braids that she wore the rest of the week, and it fell on her back, an undulating mass.

I took off my sandals and quickened my pace to walk ahead of the group. Then Kasia called me. "Hey, Yanka, don't walk so fast. Don't you want to walk with all of us together?"

"No, I want to walk alone, ahead of everybody. I want to make footprints, you know, like the footprints in *Robinson Crusoe*" (one of the books my father read to me when I was at home).

"You want to make footprints? Is that why you took off your shoes?"

"Yes! But see, my sandals didn't get dirty. And I will wash my feet before putting them back on."

Kasia shakes her head. She doesn't understand.

I want to see my footprints. I want to see what marks I make in the soft brown earth. I want everyone to know I was here!

Twelve o'clock Mass. The Big Mass they call it, longest of the day. I dip my hand in the urn filled with Holy Water to cross myself before I settle next to Halinka in the very front pew. I notice Poldziu, who serves as altar boy. I cannot take my eyes off him. He is so handsome! He moves with grace, bringing and taking away, assisting at Mass. I envy him his beautiful vestments, his cassock with all that lace, and his role at the altar. He is so important.

I remember myself onstage in Krakow and Tarnopol. I would like to be part of this play. The incense intoxicates me. I love the smell. I inhale, close my eyes, and get dizzy from holding my breath.

Everything about church is exciting. The deeper religious meaning escapes me at this point. I feel like I am in the theatre. Everyone knows their parts so well, even the audience. We sing in one voice, always on cue (not even remotely resembling prayer in a synagogue).

During the sermon, Poldziu turns around and winks at me. I lower my head and steal a glance at Farmer Kaza, to see if he has noticed his son flirting with me. But Kaza hasn't seen anything. He is sitting hat in hand, staring at Poldziu, his youngest son, with such pride that his large, bony face is twisted into a foolish smile.

Kaza is a neighbor. He has a very small farm and a very large family. All the farmers help one another, but we have to hire men from among the peasants to do the work on our farm. The two oldest Kaza boys work here every day. Sofia is the housemaid, and Basia, her youngest sister, comes with Poldziu on Sundays, after church, to help in the kitchen.

Sunday, after church, is the big weekly reception. The number of people varies, but Professor Siodmak, Dr. Krawczyk, and Father Groszka have never missed the big feast. We have food on the farm. Professor Siodmak brings carbide for our lamps. There is none in the village store, only in the city, if you know where to find it. Dr. Krawczyk brings medicines, especially aspirin, which is impossible to obtain. His blonde wife, Maria, a friend of Pani Ala's, never comes without a shiny satin *bonbonnière* full of divine chocolates, which we await—with the greatest anticipation—to be invited to share after lunch.

The priest is a friend of the family, has been for many years. He comes often for a sip of vodka and conversation. Father Groszka, as all the rest of the villagers, treats the professor with deference and admiration. Today the father brought with him a young priest we had never seen before.

Father Francishek is his name. He wears brown robes, not black like Father Groszka, and I wonder why.

Father Francishek looks very young; that surprises me also. I thought all priests were old men. He's young and looks very strong, but not like a peasant. He's tall and broad-shouldered and handsome as well. I like the way he looks at Magda. I like his black eyes, mocking all the time. One of his teeth, the canine on the right, catches his lip when he smiles. He looks like he's biting it as he ponders something. Magda has monopolized him; there is no doubt about that. She and the young priest are flirting. He must be telling her only amusing stories because she is laughing all the time.

I maneuver to sit next to him at lunch. I want to know him better. There is something about him I like very much. Anyway, he told me he hopes I will come to his catechism class.

The Sunday meal is slow and leisurely. It takes time to consume all the courses. The men drink vodka first, with salty herring tidbits. Eggs chopped with onions that have been stuffed back into the half-shells are served as a first course on a bed of lettuce. Then comes soup and roast pork with sauerkraut and beans.

I remember, when I first came to live on the farm, how I worried about eating pork. I would not eat meat for months, only rabbit and chicken. Then one day I forgot and ate the roasted pork loin, which from then on became my favorite meat.

Potatoes are a staple that we eat with everything. For dessert there is vanilla pudding, and a "placek"—sort of a tart encrusted with fruit. Imitation coffee (made of roasted grains and chicory) is served on the veranda on Sundays. It is there that the men go to smoke and drink and talk about the war.

On the veranda, a large map of Europe covers the only wall in this large glassed-in room. It draws the men like a magnet. They stand around it and point and argue and discuss; the tone is hushed, almost inaudible. I sneak into the adjacent bedroom because I want to know all about the war. When will it end so we can go home? Home?

Now they point to the right, where it says "Russia." Father Francishek explains, in an agitated manner, about the difficulties the Germans have encountered on the Russian front. Glancing around to be assured he is safe and no one is listening, he says, "The Germans will be beaten. You will see!"

Not much is known about the conditions on the Eastern front, but Father Francishek has information that gives him hope. The Germans will not win this war. I like what he is saying.

I can wait no longer. I want to be on the veranda and talk about the war.

I am allowed to stay only for a short visit; then Pan Professor sends me to the well to bring some fresh cold water.

In the kitchen I say to Poldziu, "Come help me get some fresh water from the well." A good enough excuse to have Poldziu with me.

All the visitors leave at dusk—never without tea and a short recital of Chopin or Bach given by Pani Ala.

CHAPTER 16

Our First Winter
on the Farm

I expected something special to happen, some sign, some kind of warning. We talked about it long enough. But . . . despite the evening frosts and chilly mornings, winter comes suddenly! One morning it's here! It came during the night! The familiar landscape is gone. The snow has covered everything. Nothing looks the same.

I stand a long time by the open door, looking at the courtyard. I don't want to go out. The whiteness hurts my eyes and I feel it would be almost sacrilegious to mar it with my footsteps. Winter seems so different here on the farm. No color anywhere. Only black and white. When the sun shines, the barren branches make shadows on the smooth, glistening snow, and when the wind rises a little, they look like strange abstract drawings, moving slowly on a giant white canvas.

I stare with fascination at all this whiteness and wonder what would happen if I threw some color on it.

In the next few days, the snow is so abundant we build a giant snowman. He will stand near the window for the rest of the winter.

Each season on the farm is a new experience for both Gaby and me. A lot of work that has to be done indoors has been set aside for winter.

The beans have been stored in the attic, vines and all, to dry. Also, green and yellow peas. We work in the small kitchen where it is warm. We sit on low stools. Leshek brings a bale of beans from the attic. The pods are hard and brittle—with one squeeze they open, letting out a stream of hard, dried beans onto the apron on my lap.

We husk the pintos and the limas, the green and yellow peas, and stack the burlap bags, filled to the brim, in the dark, cool corners of the storage pantry.

And, while working, we sing. I learn new songs that boys sing to girls when they are in love.

More snow fell and stayed on the ground. The days got shorter and I listened to everyone who had stories to tell about Christmas. I was an ardent and devout Catholic by now, but I hadn't ever celebrated Christmas.

Halinka wanted to go look for a tree.

"Yanka, come! We will find a tree, here at the end of the garden. There are lots of them there, I am sure we can find a nice one. We will put a ribbon around it and tell Leshek to cut it. Come!"

"I'm so glad you asked me to go with you. It's my first Christmas ever. You know, I have never had a Christmas tree?"

"You haven't? Why not?" She looked at me, puzzled.

"I—I don't know." Immediately I realized I'd made a terrible blunder. I tried to invent a story to cover it up. How could I have forgotten?

But Halinka didn't pay any attention to me. She ran to tell her father that she wanted to find this year's Christmas tree.

"You cannot go alone into the woods to look for a tree," said Pan Professor.

"Oh, no, Papa, we're not going into the woods. We will find it here at the edge of the garden."

"You cannot cut any of those trees. They protect the house from the road."

"I know, but one tree less will not make a difference."

"Oh, yes it will. Anyway, the prettiest spruces are down by the other well, near the fishponds. There is a patch of trees there, thick and straight. Just what you need to make a beautiful Christmas tree."

We found the perfect one. When it finally stood mounted in the salon by the piano, we began decorating it with the cookies we had baked a couple of days before. We had Santa Clauses, and stars, and angels to which we glued faces and costumes made of paper decals. We hung green and red apples, and yellowish pears, and a few candies in colorful wrappers.

The night before Christmas Eve we sat in the small winter kitchen way into the night making a paper chain—very colorful and many meters long—and we draped it all around the tree. On the very top sat an angel.

Finally, the tree stood all dressed and majestic, the candleholders clipped to the ends of the branches. Christmas Eve was the next day. We would light them just before *Vigilia* (the traditional Christmas Eve meal), and then it would be a sight to behold.

I could hardly wait, and I wondered why we had never had a Christmas tree at home.

Just before Christmas Eve many people came with season's greetings. Farmer Kaza's wife brought a country pâté made of pheasant and duck. Some others brought fruit jams or even cakes and cookies. I do not remember if we gave them anything in return, but there was friendly chitchat, and glasses full of vodka were raised *"to good health and Merry Christmas"*. If it wasn't snowing, more people came to visit.

Mieczyslaw, or Mietek as everyone called him, is the local forester. He came to tell about the wounded boar he found entangled in bramble bushes. He sat with Pan Professor on the veranda, drinking and puffing on the pipe he was clenching between his teeth even when he talked.

I had seen Mietek before. You couldn't have missed him, even in a crowd. He was taller than most, his hair was bright red, and his nose and cheeks were covered with a thousand freckles. He is always dressed in rough wool tweeds and riding boots. Every Sunday he stands across the street from church, leaning against a tree, looking at Kasia as she slowly and cautiously descends the steps because she's not at ease in the high-heeled shoes she wears to Mass on Sunday.

She knows he has eyes for her and that makes her shy and nervous. She passes him by quickly. With a nod, she acknowledges his presence. He smiles, tips his hat, and continues staring at her while puffing on his pipe. Even though they rarely speak, you can tell by their looks they are attracted to each other.

Mietek is on the veranda, talking to Kasia's father. She waited in the small winter kitchen until she heard him leaving. Then she came into the big vestibule and wished him a Merry Christmas. He is halfway out the door, hesitating before he closed it, when she blurted out the invitation to the biggest party ever—the one of St. Sylvester, the last night of the old year.

Vigilia, the grand twelve-course dinner on Christmas Eve, is a family affair. It is served very slowly, so that we finish eating just in time to leave for midnight Mass. Then, stuffed with food and drink, we all piled into the large sled, and with the bells ringing, we sang Christmas carols all the way to church.

Oh, what a spectacle—the birth of Christ the Lord. The music, the crèche, the feeling of a miracle happening right there. I singing my heart out, welcoming the Lord.

The rest of the week we cleaned, cooked, and baked, preparing for the party on the thirty-first of December, when everyone comes together to celebrate.

The vodka was flowing and there was more food than I had ever seen. There was a party in every part of the house. The big kitchen, which was used in the winter only to bake bread, was full of young people singing and dancing to the whining sounds of the accordions, which were played by the Krupki twins, who came from the village just beyond.

I moved from room to room, observing. I had never seen such a party. It was all unfamiliar and exciting.

Wojtek and Malgosia were huddled on the floor by the bread oven, looking like a pretzel, their arms intertwined. His head was in her blouse, hers on the back of his neck, and both of them were giggling, or something that sounded like it, grinning, and sighing with pleasure.

Baffled and ashamed to witness such strange passion, I didn't know what to do with myself. So I went searching for Halinka, who, like me, was still considered a child and not allowed to drink.

I looked into the small winter kitchen and saw Kasia and Mietek absorbed with one another. Mietek was bent forward, his elbows on his knees, tapping his foot to the music coming from the big kitchen next door, and looking straight into Kasia's eyes so intensely that I was sure he was romancing her even though I couldn't hear what he was saying. Eavesdropping was impolite but I couldn't help myself. Since no one paid any attention to me, and Gaby was nowhere to be found . . . I amused myself by listening in on everyone's conversations.

I finally found Halinka in the salon by the Christmas tree, flirting with Janek Siodmak, who was a bit older and looking very shy. Here the conversations were subdued and the guests did not look drunk. Father Francishek was talking to Magda again, excitedly explaining something about the war. He always talked about the war and never about religion. He must have been saying something important because she was mesmerized, looking at his mouth, drinking every word as if it were some exotic nectar.

All of this was very disconcerting to me because he was a priest. But tonight the world was upside-down anyway. Servants drank with all the other guests. Professor Siodmak danced with Sofia, and Pani Ala laughed all night and even looked soft and tender.

These festivities did not end with the dawn of January but continued until everyone was sober and able to go home.

✳ ✳ ✳

That first winter was the best that I can remember. Gaby was working with Leshek, learning about horses. By now he knew how to apply cooked linseed to an infected horse's leg, and he knew how to dress it. He was brushing down the chestnut mare. She was a gentle horse, and he even helped with the shoeing.

Gaby much preferred to be with the animals or in the barn shoveling hay than at the piano, where he was forced to practice for at least an hour a day. We liked working together whenever possible, and while we were on the farm I don't think we ever had a fight. On the contrary; at night we huddled in bed, scratching each other's backs. We confided in each other. Under the covers, in secret, we complained about our lot and gave each other courage. Sometimes together we plotted revenge.

Together we fed the pigs. Gaby helped me carry the heavy wooden pales filled with cooked potato peelings that we fed our sows when they had been bred and were in gestation. He had to bring in wood for the kitchen stove from the woodshed, and I had to collect the eggs.

Most of our chickens laid their eggs where they were supposed to, in the chicken coop, where there was straw and the eggs were easy to find. But there were two or three ornery old birds that insisted on laying their eggs in the most inaccessible places where only an acrobat could find them. That was one of my responsibilities, as was feeding and milking the cows.

In winter, most of the farm work was done from dawn till about midday; the afternoons were devoted to lessons.

Pan Professor was teaching his daughters, and they, in turn, taught us.

Pani Ala gave us piano lessons and was very demanding about practice; she made no exceptions. Everyone had to come prepared.

I was also learning Latin, simply listening in on the lessons Pan Professor was giving the girls in the small winter kitchen, where I sat by the stove and peeled potatoes for dinner.

No one, not even my father, had been aware of my special talent for language, any language. I had learned to count in French, one day at the circus, when I was three. From my Viennese governess I learned German; from my ballet teacher, Russian. Now it was Latin, and Pan Professor was always surprised when I would prompt one of his daughters, whispering to them the correct word when they were unable to come up with the answer. Every once in a while he would reprimand me and tell me to be quiet, not to disturb his lessons. But most of the time he was proud of me and pleased that I was learning Latin, even though he had not taught me.

In the evenings, we sat together in the small kitchen—which was always the warmest room in the house—by the harsh light of the hissing carbide lamp, reading or sewing, darning stockings, or repairing torn bed linen.

After the first of the year, began the most awaited social event: feather stripping. In the foothills of the Tatra Mountains, where winters are terribly harsh, all the feathers and down are saved to be made later into thick featherbeds or comforters and pillows. But first the feathers have to be sorted. Everybody in the village saved their feathers for the time when all the young people will get together and go as a group to all the farms and strip, sort, and clean the feathers.

Ours was always the first house where they started, at the very beginning of January. All the young men and women came every evening, sitting in a big circle, and while they worked stripping and sorting the feathers, they sang. Sometimes they sang fashionable love songs, or old folk ballads; occasionally the men told dirty jokes, full of double meanings, and the girls giggled and gossiped.

Very often these young people brought friends from other villages, especially if there were pretty girls in the group. And it didn't take long for some of them to fall in love; by the time they were finished with the business of the feathers, many of them were engaged or seriously courting.

When the work was all done, there was the traditional party, the best party of the year, better even than St. Sylvester because there were only young people. Sometimes it went on for days, until all the food was gone and there was not a drop of vodka left. Then they slept. You could find them anywhere: in the barn, in the stables, anywhere they fell.

For me, one of those parties was quite unforgettable. They almost killed me with their bimber, homemade vodka. Leshek was drunk—so drunk that he must not have known what he was doing when he forced me to drink bimber—twice as strong as the kind you got at the store.

He insisted I try it. He said I was the only one who had remained sober, and that, he said, wasn't fair. Since I considered myself to be almost grown up (I smoked oak leaves with the boys in secret), I could drink some bimber when I was invited to do so.

No sooner had I swallowed this foul-tasting firewater than my insides convulsed and I began to vomit.

I had never been so sick in all my life, and if there was ever a time when I wanted to die, this was it. Afterward, I couldn't even tolerate the smell of alcohol without becoming ill.

CHAPTER 17

The Germans Come for Tea

They came on horseback.

They appeared in the garden without any warning. They rode single file, slowly, as if they were out for a stroll. The naked trees did not shield them from view. They made dark holes in the white snow. I knew immediately why they were coming! I watched them dismount and tie up the horses. Through the open door of the stable I saw them walking up the steps to the house, into the vestibule, where the darkness engulfed them.

I knew why they were here. I knew it right away. Someone had denounced us! They came to arrest us and take us away. Maybe they would kill us all, the professor for hiding Jews, and us for . . . no reason I knew or understood.

A giant wave of nausea glides over me like some unctuous syrup, clinging to my entrails. I wish I could vomit, get rid of this feeling. Its fear, I know. I will hide! I am not going to let them take me! I have time to escape! The back window, through which we shovel out the manure—big enough for me to pass through—and then down to the woods. I will run and hide in the trees. They will never find me. They will not know where to look. I have a plan in my head . . . I know a tree . . . but what about my brother? Where is he? I cannot go alone and leave him.

I run across the courtyard to the back of the house, and sneak into the kitchen.

"Where is Gaby?" I ask.

"Never mind where he is. Where have *you* been? Will you please tell me?" Sofia is angry! "Where have you been? I looked for you everywhere! We have to serve tea. Come help me prepare the canapés; the Germans are waiting."

I think she doesn't know they came for me, to take me. She doesn't understand! She doesn't know about me. But I said nothing. With trembling hands, I cut and spread and do what I am told. Better not attract any kind of attention now. One tray is set with the tea service, the other with food.

"I will carry in the tea," Sofia says. "It is heavier. You follow behind me with the food tray."

"Sofia! I can't! I can't!"

"Why not?"

"I am afraid!"

"Afraid of what—the soldiers?"

"Yes, of course, the soldiers. I am afraid of them! Not you?"

"They came to meet Pan Professor. They know he speaks German, so the commandant of this area came himself to greet him. There is no reason for you to be afraid! Anyway, Pani Ala told me not to be afraid."

I don't trust her at all, but I have no choice. Pani Ala enters the kitchen and immediately shouts at me. "Where have you been? You are never where you are needed. Now, hurry up and bring in the food tray, and when you serve the colonel, you curtsy with one knee and smile! Why are you looking at me as if I were a ghost?"

Sofia enters first, carrying the heavy tray. I follow, trying to hide behind her bulky body. The room is too bright! Flooded by three streams of sunrays coming through the windows, the reflection of the white landscape outside makes it even brighter. I have to squint, and it hurts my unbelieving eyes!

The scene is completely unreal. Pani Ala is holding the cut crystal glass in her hand, the little finger extended elegantly, tilting her head in the direction of the colonel, who is smiling and obviously flirting with her. Pan Professor is engrossed in conversation with the fat, blond, older German, who is also smiling.

I am in shock. My eyes must be deceiving me, or maybe I am dreaming. Are these Gestapo just ordinary men, who can make polite conversation and have a drink with the Kluszewskis as if they were the best of friends?

Strange, this scene, very strange! The strangest scene I have ever witnessed. I have never seen Gestapo sit and speak quietly with smiles on their faces. They look just like all the other guests who have come to this house. They don't look like they want us.

I stand in front of the colonel and present the tray with the canapés. My eyes are downcast. I cannot look at him, not yet. I am still petrified. He might see the panic in my eyes.

I forget to curtsy. Pani Ala gives my arm a pinch and I remember, and genuflect like in church and then move on to serve the others.

Pan Professor smiles when I am before him and then touches my arm and winks. His face is kind. Everyone is on their best behavior.

Magda, who is always talking, stands quietly by the window with a frozen smile on her parted lips.

Three times around, I am told to go. Thank God it's over! I am safely back in the kitchen.

Later, when the Germans had gone, Pan Professor told me what the colonel said.

"He was boasting about making this country 'Jude-Rein'—you understand what that means? He was telling me we should be grateful to the Fuhrer for this great favor. Cleaning up Poland once and for all.

"He was very proud of having become so adept at ferreting out Jews; he could almost smell them, he said. 'Well,' I said to myself, 'we will let you smell our little Yanka, and see!'"

"Why?" I ask. "Why did you do this? Did you want them to take us away and kill us?"

"No! I wanted to show you that you should not be afraid, that you really are Yanka Lesiak."

Was this a new game? Was he telling me that I was really Yanka Lesiak now? Did it mean that I had really changed? Or was he saying that I was safe because I looked like an Aryan? I was Yanka Lesiak, Aryan, blonde, blue-eyed, and Catholic! Maybe it was true.

After that first time the Germans came often. We cooked and served them, but I was no longer afraid. They ate and they drank, and they discussed the war with Pan Professor.

Once, to amuse them, Halinka and I were ordered to play the piano. Pani Ala chose a piece for four hands by Chopin we had been rehearsing. We were very nervous and more afraid of Pani Ala than of the Germans.

CHAPTER 18

Stefan Comes
to Run the Farm

Soon after Christmas farmers start thinking of spring. They wait for the snow to melt and the earth to thaw so they can start anew.

Even though the white blanket of a recent snowfall still made winter present, our thoughts were on planting. Will the warm weather come early? Will there be too much water, or maybe not enough? We waited for spring to break into the landscape.

There were no men working for us now, only Leshek, the stable boy. Pani Ala was nagging Pan Professor to hire someone to help with the farm work: a younger man who knew agriculture and who could supervise the hired help.

"I cannot do this myself," she said, "and neither can you. We have to get someone. I want to send for Stefan; he will be an excellent foreman."

But Pan Professor was very reluctant. For some unknown reason he did not want to hire this man, who was a distant relative of Pani Ala's. He resisted as long as he could. There were long discussions and loud arguments.

Finally, one day, Pani Ala had won. She announced that Stefan was coming to run the farm, week after next, just in time for spring.

On the day of his arrival, Pani Ala took the carriage and went to the station by herself.

Magda and Halina were dying of curiosity. They had never seen this Stefan, who was coming to change our lives. Pani Ala had forewarned us, "There will be changes in this house."

Myself (far left) and my Brother (far right) in pasture with the cows

We had heard that Stefan was an agronomist. His parents had suffered financial reversals before the war, they lost their property, and now he was obliged to go to work for someone else.

It was rumored that he was handsome, and a bachelor, something that bothered Kasia, who was secretly in love with Mietek.

He arrived from the station in a heavy green overcoat and a wide-rimmed green felt hat. A long woolen muffler was wound around the collar, making his face almost invisible.

Everyone came into the vestibule to welcome him. Pan Professor stayed on the veranda and I behind the door in the small winter kitchen.

When he peeled off his outer clothing, I noticed his black, shiny riding boots, and they made me think of the Gestapo. The skin on his face was stretched tightly over the high cheekbones. His cheeks were red, his eyes beady, and his nostrils pinched. The mouth was a thin, straight red line, like a cut across the bottom of the face just before the chin. He looked mean.

Pani Ala had ordered us to prepare a very special meal. As soon as they arrived from the station, we head for the table. This was our opportunity to observe Stefan while he talked about his plans. Abruptly, Pan Professor interrupted Stefan midsentence and told him what he expected of him as a foreman.

After he finished eating, Stefan asked to be shown around the property. He saw the gardens first. In the stables he checked out the horses. He made comments about everything: that the farm had been neglected was his overall conclusion.

There was much to do, and he was here to do it. The very next day, he hired Jack, a shy, strapping young farmer who was glad to get the work.

Stefan examined the plows, the seeding machine, and the mill; he wanted all the tools and equipment repaired so when the time came he would be able to use them.

Stefan was given the small room upstairs, directly above ours. I could hear him every morning. He was up before dawn. He wanted the stables cleaned and the horses fed before he came to inspect them.

The work on the farm had always been hard, but now Stefan demanded more from everybody. He ran the farm like a military camp. Whether he was on foot or on horseback, the riding crop never left his hand. He mercilessly whipped his horse and constantly struck the side of his right boot while he gave out orders.

We were all afraid of him, even Kasia, who one day said to me in great confidence, "I hate this man who invaded our home and took over our farm, but, I have to admit, the farm has not been run so efficiently in years."

Pretty soon even Pan Professor had to admit that Stefan was a very good foreman and that things had improved greatly since he took over the work on the farm.

Only nobody liked him.

One evening Stefan came into the small winter kitchen where I was finishing the washing of the dinner dishes. No one else was there, only him and me. He asked me point blank why we had come to live with Pan Professor

The tone of his voice frightened me, and I wondered why he was asking me those questions. Not knowing what to do, I remained silent.

"Why don't you want to answer me?" he asked, looking straight at me.

"I . . . I will answer you, of course. It's just that I thought you knew. Being in the family, I thought Pan Professor had told you."

"He did tell me a story. He said that your parents were lost in a bombing, in Lwow. Is that how it happened?"

"Yes," I said, but I was petrified. I thought he either suspects or he knows something about us.

"Well . . . well, I didn't know Kluszewski had any relatives in Lwow."

Since I had been afraid of him from the start, I had always tried very hard to stay out of his way as much as possible; now I considered running away into the woods to live with the Partisans.

It was a very serious thought, but first I decided to confide in Kasia. I had to tell someone about my encounter with Stefan the previous evening, and of the questions he had asked me.

"You must never leave me alone with him again," I said to Kasia. "He really scares me to death."

"Yanka, you must tell my father everything you have just told me. He must know that Stefan has been questioning you. I for one don't know anything about Stefan. I don't know who he is or what he did before he came here. All I know is that he is a distant relative of my mother's."

"Why do you think he asked where we came from? Do you think he suspects something?"

"I don't know what to think. All I know is that he is a creep. Can you imagine he told my mother that he wants to marry me?"

"Oh, my God! What did Pani Ala say to him?"

"I don't know what she told him, I only know what she told me. She said she would be delighted if I would accept his proposal. I told her that will never happen because I can't stand him. Not his looks or his behavior. My mother was shocked! She thinks he is extremely good-looking.

"We must tell my father about all this. Maybe he will do something about Stefan. Maybe he will get rid of him. Personally, I think he is dangerous, especially to Gaby."

So I was right. This was serious, something new for me to worry about. An enemy within, living right here in the house.

Kasia and I went to see Pan Professor on the veranda and we told him both our stories. He was very perturbed, especially since Kasia had refused Stefan's proposal of marriage so bluntly.

But Pan Professor had other reasons to be suspicious about Stefan.

When the Germans had put out an edict about food, which had to be delivered "on contingent" to help the war effort, they first inventoried all the farms. Then they started confiscating. Every month we had to deliver a calf, or a pig, or chickens. At the end they even took a cow.

But at the beginning, what the Germans wanted most were pigs. So when a sow had been bred and was in gestation, they had a record of it. They knew there would soon be a litter.

When the piglets were born, inspectors came and put earrings with a number on each pig; this way the animals were registered and identifiable.

Some months later the orders would come from the local commandatur, in the form of a letter, as to where and when the hog with the earring number so-and-so was to be delivered. And every week, hundreds of these animals were brought to the yard near the station, from where they were shipped out to who-knows-where to feed the Germans so they could win the war. The pigs were kept together in a giant pen, where they screamed and fought and bit each other's ears.

Leshek was struggling with the pig we had just brought in. It had been inspected and checked off and stamped. The official receipt for the delivery was in our hands, when Leshek noticed someone else's pig screaming with pain, its ear torn in half and the earring hanging loose. He looked around to make sure that nobody was watching and carefully reached over, pulled the earring off, and put it in his pocket. We were now in possession of a plain metal earring with a number that had been crossed off the German inventory. An earring no jewel could ever match in value. With it we would be able to steal one of our own pigs and raise it for ourselves. Stefan was adamantly against it.

At the time we had two sows on the farm, Baba and Malucha. Baba was a normal pig. Malucha was a giant. When she was in gestation her belly was so enormous it hung to the ground. She was the most prolific producer we had on the farm. One time she had a litter of eighteen pigs, and all were born alive. But she was a mean sow and we had to keep her in a separate pen. When she was ready to give birth, we watched her day and night because she was known to eat her young, especially the smaller ones. That was going to be the excuse we would give the Germans in case they took the trouble to count her swollen nipples.

In the meantime, we hid the biggest and healthiest piglet until the German inspector branded and registered the rest of the litter. Then, with our stolen earring clipped onto our pig's ear, we made it indistinguishable by putting it in the pen with all the other piglets. It would have been very difficult for anyone who was looking casually to notice that, among all those pigs, there was one with a false earring on its ear.

But we knew our piglet well and tended it with very special care. To fatten it up faster we fed it separately with special food. It grew big and fat and we waited with anticipation for the day that we could eat it. No one was a bit sentimental. Food was food.

At the time when we brought home the earring, Stefan was the only one who objected. He warned about the consequences that could be expected for stealing from the Germans.

No one paid any attention to him then, but now when it finally came time to slaughter our pig for the upcoming holidays, we knew we had to be very careful and take special precautions. Preparations had to be made. Everything had to be done with the utmost secrecy. All the work had to be finished in one night—the slaughtering, the cooking, the sausage-making, and the smoking. The smoking was particularly dangerous. The smoke could travel far, and it could lead to discovery.

To avoid suspicion and to confuse the scent, they built other fires all around the smokehouse where they burned pinecones and other pungent wood, which completely obliterated the smell of meat from the smokehouse.

By morning there was not a trace of anything that might have suggested any kind of butchering. What had not been used was buried in the garden and the spot was well covered.

Only such friends who could really be trusted had been asked to help.

On the night of the slaughter, Stefan exploded. He was so furious that we thought he would, himself, denounce us to the Gestapo. He accused Pan Professor of endangering everyone's lives—especially his life—which he was not prepared to lose for the sake of a slaughtered pig.

After that night, everyone wondered if he was really such a coward, or if he was sympathetic to the Germans. Some went as far as to suspect him of being a Nazi.

What to do about Stefan became the big problem. Pan Professor and Pani Ala were not exactly the most harmonious or the most loving couple. They were seldom of one mind. Those who sided with Pan Professor certainly hoped he would find a way to dismiss Stefan without consequences; all the others were afraid of Pani Ala.

The pig had been slaughtered, the meat preserved and hidden. The stolen earring went on the ear of a new piglet.

Stefan was still among us, in a foul and angry mood. So far he hadn't gone to the Gestapo and hadn't reported our clandestine activities.

Since it had been raining steadily for weeks, and the fields were muddy and the pastures wet, Stefan decided this would be a good time to go and visit his parents.

He packed a great big basket with foods, including bacon and sausages, to take with him, and we all bitterly resented it.

With so much dampness, what grain we had left was swelling. The potatoes set aside for planting were rotting in the cellar.

But mushrooms were growing everywhere. By the road, in the garden where there had been trees, and in the woods—they were growing before our very own eyes.

Every day we came home, drenched to the bone, with giant baskets full of mushrooms of all sizes, colors, and varieties. The redcaps and brown boletus were the best for drying. The rest we cooked and ate. Every day Kasia invented a new way to serve mushrooms. Over mashed potatoes, over cooked barley, in soup, heaped on a thick slice of bread. There was one variety we grilled right on top of the stove and ate with salt and nothing else.

Finally the sun shined and dried the soggy land. Stefan came back. We were way behind in planting. The ground was still pretty wet, but he decided to spread the manure and try to plow anyway. Some of the vegetables would do well in wet soil.

Jack and Leshek were working the manure pile behind the stables, loading the steaming fertilizer into the wagon.

They had unhitched the horses but left them in the harness to graze. Stefan asked me to help him hitch the team back to the wagon. He was pulling on the reins, trying to back up the horses, while I was supposed to hitch them to the wagon.

I don't know why one of the horses reared and the other one pulled forward, but the wagon jackknifed, the tongue between the horses broke, and the wagon turned over. The manure spilled all over the garden, and one of the horses broke a leg.

Stefan flew into an uncontrollable rage. He screamed like a madman. With his riding crop he struck me on the head and then again across the bridge of my nose. I heard the crunch more than I felt it. Then nothing, just blackness.

To revive me, he threw water in my face. When I came to, Stefan told me to go into the house and wash up!

Hardly able to breathe, choking on the warm blood running down my throat and gushing out of my nostrils, I held my nose in both hands and ran to the well in the courtyard. Near the well, the big cement trough was filled with water for the animals. I stuck my head in the trough to bathe it in the cool, clear water.

I held my breath, opened my eyes, and watched in fascination my blood invade the water, like some kind of monster with a thousand tentacles. It flowed and mixed in and then dissolved, and there was no more water, just blood.

I am drowning, I thought while slowly bleeding to death through my nose.

When they pulled me out, my face had swollen beyond recognition.

The rest of that day is vague. Cold compresses and pain. Excruciating pain. Dr. Krawczyk came and did something to my nose; I don't know what. I couldn't see. I couldn't eat or drink and I couldn't breathe. My mouth was dry all the time. My face was black and blue and swollen. I looked grotesque.

Then from blue it slowly turned to yellow and faded back to normal. When the swelling was all gone, I had a new bump on the side of my nose.

Nobody ever mentioned anything about that day, as if it had never existed. As if nothing had ever happened. Only Stefan left and never returned.

CHAPTER 19

I'm so Happy; This Sunday
Is My First Communion

After the accident everyone was nice to me, even Pani Ala. She took me to her bedroom and gave me Halinka's first communion dress. Halinka had finally outgrown it. I had coveted that dress, which was made of white linen organdie, for years. It was the most beautiful dress I had ever seen. It had pleats and ruffles, and a white satin cummerbund. Finally it was mine.

I had been preparing for my first communion for months. This week I went to confession for the first time. On Sunday during the big morning Mass, dressed in white from head to toe, a beautiful candle in my hand, I received communion for the first time—little white wafer, the Body of Christ.

Good-bye, child! In the eyes of God, I was an adult now, responsible for my sins, which I would have to confess and atone for, myself. I had never before felt so important.

At Easter, during the procession, I was a flower girl—strewing petals from the little basket suspended from my neck, signing myself, and genuflecting after every step.

There were only two of us, Barbara and me. We threw flowers in the path of the Father, who was carrying the cross monstrance, and then we genuflected and stepped back. We set the pace for the whole procession since we had to kneel and walk backwards.

It was indeed a great honor for the family that I was chosen to be a flower girl in the Easter procession. I had finally done something that pleased Pani Ala.

★ ★ ★

It is almost summer, the sun is shining, and the sky seems higher and bluer. There are no clouds. The air is hot; it waves and dances in front of my eyes.

In the south pasture, with my cows, I'm lying on my back, chewing on a blade of grass and daydreaming. A fly stops on my nose; my eyes cross to observe it. The song of birds from the nearby forest and the rhythmic whipping of the cows' tails, forever chasing off bloodthirsty insects, are the only noises around.

Since my cows are behaving, grazing with contentment, I can think of boys. More and more now I think about boys. I too want to be in love. I am very curious; *how does it feel when one is in love?* I wonder. Will I have to tell the boy the truth about myself when I fall in love? A very faint and distant sound distracts me from my daydreams, as if it were the hum of a thousand bumblebees. I shield my eyes with my hand and try to keep them open as I look up at the sky. There are twenty or thirty or maybe more tiny silver birds gliding in formation. One . . . two . . . three . . . four . . . I count. Suddenly, the antiaircraft guns start pounding. The sky is filled with white puffs of smoke. A hit. An explosion!

The wounded one is on the way down, spewing black smoke and red flames like an angry dragon. Spinning as he falls to earth, growing bigger and bigger, he comes down somewhere over the hill beyond the forest, yonder out of sight.

The guns have stopped.

The airplanes are gone. From the blue sky, five white balloons are gliding down in silence. Five men are dangling from the white parachutes. Then they too are gone. Fallen out of sight.

The Germans are everywhere. Motorcycles with sidecars and all kinds of vehicles speed by, yelling, shouting, searching the woods.

The news spreads like wildfire!

One dead. Three captured. One they can't find.

A brisk trade in parachute fabric follows. No one knows what it is, no one has ever seen or heard of nylon, but they like it; even though they could be arrested, they buy it and sell it just to own a piece—a piece of something that came from America. They think that if it fell from the sky, it had to be a good omen.

Afterward for weeks, the subject on everyone's lips was the *Americans* who came down from the sky. Fantastic stories about them grew as the incident itself faded from memory. And no one knew what happened to the airmen—the one who disappeared and the three whom they had captured. They were our unknown heroes.

We spun tales about the Americans: They were preparing to conquer the Germans from the sky. One day soon they will come back, and they will drop from the sky and ride down on their shiny white parachutes to set us free.

Father Francishek said the airplanes were on their way to bomb the oil fields of Ploesti, in Rumania, but I preferred to believe they were planning our rescue.

One day, Stashek, the redhead from Kovalski's farm, started fighting with me about the Americans. He said they could never fly as far as Poland, and I said they could. It escalated from words to a fistfight when Gaby told Stashek he would not allow him to insult his sister—and then got up and punched Stashek in the stomach.

Stashek grabbed Gaby by the neck and threw him to the ground. They rolled and rolled around, pummeling each other, when suddenly Stashek jumped up and ran screaming into the woods. While rolling around, the boys had ripped open a wasp's nest, and the angry wasps were swarming, attacking everyone—especially the cows, which spooked and ran straight for the trees. It took us hours to find them and bring them back to pasture.

Stashek was badly stung by the wasps and his face was swelling, so he ran home to his mother.

Gaby had a bloody nose, a sore stomach and back, and a few stings as well, but he was a hero. My little baby brother was no baby anymore.

Not so long ago, he was still such a little boy. I was so worried about him. He was always hungry. When there was no fruit on the trees or berries or mushrooms in the woods, I didn't know what to do to feed him, and I worried when he cried because he was so hungry.

I remember the time I was caught stealing potatoes too early in the season. I had pulled out whole plants to pick off a few potatoes and left the plants on the ground nearby. Those plants had many more tiny potatoes attached to their roots, which would have become big had they been left to grow in the ground. For doing such a wasteful thing, I got a severe beating.

I should have thrown those plants far away from here so no one would know that I pulled them out, I thought. Then I realized there would have been visible holes where the plants had been growing. And probably I would have been punished anyway. I had to find a new way to steal potatoes, since they were the best food to assuage our hunger.

In the fall, when mornings were damp and cold, we often lit a fire. We baked potatoes in the fire and kept our hands and feet warm.

I had to think of another way to get those potatoes out of the ground without getting caught. One day while I was weeding, working with a small hoe, I noticed there were strange bumps on the side of the furrows that had not been there the last time. By scratching away the earth, I found that these bumps were large potatoes that were growing outward. I stuck my hands into the softened earth and found many more right beneath the surface. I felt for the largest ones and pulled them off the root; then I patted the ground around the plant so no one could ever suspect that this particular plant had started with more potatoes on it.

After the potatoes had been harvested, we baked sugar beets; then they were out of the ground and there was nothing to be found in the fields or in the forests.

Uncle Mooniu had been wrong. We were now hungry, even on the farm.

Pan Professor and Pani Ala ate behind closed doors so none of us would know they had hidden food for themselves that they did not want to share with the rest of the household.

We baked the same amount of loaves of bread, but the loaves were smaller. We each got one slice of bread per day, where before it had been unlimited. And Gaby always wanted more.

One Sunday after the reception, I was clearing the dishes when I noticed a large heel of bread that had been left on the table by our guests. I decided to steal it and hide it for Gaby; he could eat it later under the covers in bed. On the way to the kitchen, I stuck it into our straw mattress, where I hid everything I didn't want anyone to find.

A few days later, Gaby was complaining that he was hungry.

"Don't cry," I said, "I've got some bread for you!" I dug into the mattress and brought out the bread.

Unfortunately, the bread had dried and hardened, and we could neither cut it nor break it nor bite it. Gaby was very angry with me. What to do now to make it soft again?

"I'll soak it in water." But that didn't work either. I had to find a dish and then a place to hide the dish. When I finally came back for the bread, it had become so soggy it was impossible to take it out of the dish.

Aside from the Germans, food was our main preoccupation. I had to think of a way to store bread, if I ever got a chance to steal it again. *Surely there will be an opportunity,* I thought. *I must be prepared.*

I found the solution one day while cutting vegetables for soup—*that's what I will do with the bread, cut it into little cubes! Then, even dry, we can chew it. Or hold it in our mouths and wait until it softens.*

From then on, any piece of bread that I could steal I cut into little pieces and hid in the mattress.

Life had been reduced to the most common denominators: not to be discovered or denounced, to keep our bellies filled as often as possible, and not to die of pneumonia, a common way out of this world for many children on the farms.

When we were very hungry, we did not feel the cold, but once the belly was full, we realized quickly that we were not adequately clothed for the coming winter. We had outgrown our own clothes long ago, and the hand-me-downs were getting small and threadbare. We had wool sweaters in which the holes had been patched, and each of us had one pair of warm stockings and one pair of shoes.

From that time in spring when the ground had thawed and the mud had dried out, we went barefoot and never thought of shoes till the end of autumn, when it was so cold and damp that our feet became chapped and had to be protected. We pulled out the old shoes and were very surprised to find that our feet had also grown and could not be stuffed into last year's shoes.

The shoemaker had to take measurements for new wooden soles. The leather for the tops was to come from Shkapa, the old mare, who was so old she couldn't even get out to graze in the garden just behind the stables. But she was still with us, and her hide was on her back—and we were still barefoot!

In the early morning the dampness was hanging just above the ground, and it took hours of sunshine to dry the dew, which made innocent blades of grass as sharp as razor blades.

The pastures closest to the house had been grazed to the ground, and we had to take the cows to the pasture way down by the ponds. The lowlands were marshy and wet, and there were no dry twigs around with which to start a fire.

I was hugging Malina for warmth—she was the most docile of my cows—when I noticed steam rising from the dung that Malina had just dropped behind her. The dung looked steaming hot and my feet were frozen.

I couldn't resist, and, to Gaby's dismay, I stepped into the cow dung and stood in its warmth till I saw the next cow lift her tail.

I jumped from one pile to the next, building up a crust that looked like a shoe and protected my feet from the dampness and the cold. I did this for the rest of the morning and all the days that followed till we got new shoes.

CHAPTER 20

Now the Russians Are Chasing
out the Germans

This winter is the coldest winter of my life—colder than last year or ever before. Everything is frozen, even the well in the courtyard. I am cold all the time. Every time I get a chance, I sit by the stove where we burn the old stumps. Aged and hardened, they give more heat than ordinary wood.

Everybody shivers, blowing constantly on their stiffened fingers, stomping their feet to dissipate the numbness.

But there is good news. It comes from the Partisans. The Germans are losing the war!

"They had gone to Russia, and now they are coming back. Going home to Germany! Retreating!" That is what I heard the adults saying.

The main road going west reverberates with the sounds of heavy machinery. Night and day they are moving, a steady stream of trucks loaded with arms, ammunition, and men.

Soldiers! German soldiers, once so proud, so disciplined, so mean. They look cold, dejected, dull of eye, slow of speech; their uniforms torn and tattered, dirty bandages cover their wounds. They are a beaten lot, those who are going home, their arrogance lost somewhere east of here.

They dump a truckload of bullets right on our doorstep—to lighten their load, to move even faster. They want to go home! I try to imagine what it will be like when the Germans are gone. But I cannot imagine.

I can't believe what is going on in the village. Maria, one of Sofia's friends who worked for the local commandant, came to visit. She was so sorry to see her bosses leave. She had it good while working for the Germans, plenty to eat, and they even gave her clothes.

"But they told me not to come to work anymore, that they are going home to Germany, tonight," she told Sofia, crying. "Frau Gretchen took all her jewels, tied them in a linen handkerchief, and stuffed them in the crevice between her giant breasts. That's all they are taking with them, just the gold money, the jewels, and some of the paintings."

We started hearing sounds of war. The front was definitely coming our way. Every day it got a little closer, louder, and more distinct. I knew the sounds; I had heard them before. This was my third battleground, my third front, my third war.

"The Russians are in Skavina, and soon they will be here," said Father Francishek when he came to see us.

Mietek came also, with paper tape, and taped up all the windows. Every pane of glass had a paper X on it. "This way the glass will not shatter," he said.

He helped us bring water from the deep well—since the one in the courtyard was frozen—and told us to store it in the big summer kitchen.

"Do you have plenty of candles? You must be prepared in case you run out of naphtha and carbide."

I marveled at how much Mietek knew about everything, and I felt more secure when he came to look after the family; after all, we were again a household of five women, a boy, and a crippled old man.

I don't know why I was not afraid. The war was coming our way, but I had no fear of bullets, as if there was a cloud around my body no bullet could pierce. Those bullets were destined for the Germans only.

When I thought about that, I felt like there was some sort of demon swirling around inside me who was made of laughter. I could not let him out yet, but soon I would unleash him, and then we would laugh, he and I, forever.

It had stopped snowing and everything was white. The black starless night was ending and a gray, wintry dawn was peeking through the naked branches of the apple orchard. War or no war the horses had to be fed, the cows milked, and the stables cleaned.

Gaby and I both dressed under the covers before we slipped to our knees to say our morning prayers. With my eyes closed, my head bent over my folded hands, I reverently start to recite, "Our Father, who—" when sudden, loud noises stopped the prayer in my throat. I ran to the window . . . there in our courtyard was the whole German army, with trucks and cars and cannons and machine guns! There were soldiers everywhere; hundreds of them.

Now they were pounding on the door! "Open up! Open up!" they shouted in German.

Everyone runs toward the door. While the Germans are still pounding on it, Pani Ala orders us to hide in the attic. Gaby and I scramble up the ladder with Halina and Magda behind us.

I hear the Germans; they are in the house now; I hear their footsteps, and they are everywhere. Now they will surely find us.

We pulled up the ladder and closed the trap door to the attic. But they know where to look. Someone must have denounced us. This time I am sure they came here to take us. It's over now!

We sit huddled together in absolute silence, afraid to breathe, our bodies so tense we are shaking, and fear is etched on our faces. We wait and wait, but we don't hear anybody coming up the ladder.

An eternity passes until Kasia comes to fetch us. She takes us through the garden, away from all the Germans, into the master bedroom where the rest of the family is waiting.

Magda runs to her father. "What is happening? Why are they here? What do they want?"

With his hands, Pan Professor motions us to sit down. "The Germans have commandeered our house. This will be their temporary headquarters. We have been ordered to stay in this bedroom. Nobody leaves; no one comes in. Those are the orders. They have promised no harm will come to us. We have food and water that should last for a few days.

"Sofia, you who are tall, hang the thick comforter on the window; feathers are supposed to slow down the bullets. There is nothing else we can do but wait for this to be over."

I thought they had all gone back to Germany.

In the next room the operator shouts into the radio and I can hear someone shouting back, the voice fading in and out between the crackling.

We are eight people in the room and only two beds. We sleep on the floor. Since the Germans have forbidden us to leave this room, we have to use chamber pots. The outhouse is off limits.

There are German soldiers everywhere; we hear them shouting and moving about the house. Trucks rumble into and out of the courtyard. The nights are long and pitch black; the moon has been hiding. The days are short and dark gray. Night and day run into each other.

The war sounds are constant. Sometimes during the night there is an eerie silence, when the big guns have stopped. It is then that I hear the same sound every night running up and down the road: a small gun, spitting his bullets so fast I can't even count them, hunting the other one in the dark.

I have been listening for them all night. I cannot sleep. I know which one is which: the one who comes from the right is German, from the left Russian; their voices are very distinct—one enemy, one friend.

The fighting has been heavy. All day and into the night. In the room adjacent to ours I hear moaning and screaming.

Now the Germans are screaming, and we are deaf and mute. We dare not hear, we dare not speak, we dare not move out of our room. We sit silent and obedient. We wait for orders.

The stench from the chamber pots has become unbearable. We have not eaten. It doesn't matter; nobody is hungry. But we have run out of water.

The carbide lamp is not hissing anymore. The flame is pale and soft yellow, not blue as it should be. The lamp needs water. We have been in this room for days.

Pan Professor is at his wits' end. Irritated, he wants to talk to the commandant. He is almost at the door when he stops, turns around, and points his cane in my direction.

"Yanka, you will go out and bring water. They will not harm a child. Don't be afraid; just do it fast and come right back."

I cannot separate the fear from the excitement. I want to know what is happening beyond these closed doors.

Carefully I press down the handle and push the door into the other room. I tiptoe in, holding on to the handle. I try not to make any noise while closing the door behind me.

The room is lit so brightly that at first I cannot see anything. The windows are covered with dark army blankets, and on the dining table a young boy is having his leg sawed off. Everyone is silent.

There is another young soldier sitting on a chair, observing. His eyes are open and fixed. Suddenly his head falls forward and I see that the back of his skull is missing.

I am terrified! Is he alive? Is he dead? Is he waiting here for the rest of his skull? I don't want to pass by him.

The doctor who is operating looks up and waves me on. I run the rest of the way.

Later, much later, I understood why I was sent out, not Magda or Kasia. Pan Professor was afraid the older girls might get abused. But there was no need to worry, these men did not have rape on their minds.

They looked at me, those who did look, but they did not see me.

I move quickly in and out of places, gathering what I can carry. I find water in the big kitchen just where we had left it, but the rest of the house is unrecognizable. There are soldiers everywhere I go, sitting on the floor, laying on stretchers, milling about restlessly and anxiously. No one pays any attention to me. Vehicles move in and out of the courtyard, loading and unloading men. Very strange maneuvers.

I am tempted to run to the barn to look for eggs, but the yard is a black sea of mud, contrasting sharply with the snow-covered roofs of the stable and barn.

My arms are loaded. I stand in front of the closed door and do not want to reenter. No one has harmed me out here, but what about that boy in the chair with half of his skull missing? I am afraid of him! What if he moves and his brain falls out? He is a gruesome sight! Perhaps I should go back the other way, all the way around the house to the other door?

The door in front of me opens and we almost collide. The officer barks, "In or out? Make up your mind."

"In," I say, and squeeze by him. Shaking with fear, I spill water all over the floor.

Once back in the bedroom, I am bombarded with questions. Kasia brews some ersatz coffee made from roasted barley, and the scent alone is elixir for the nose. We eat hot boiled potatoes for dinner.

We stay awake all night and catnap during the day. Somehow it is better that way. But be it night or day, the sleep is never sound. At the slightest noise, we are up and listening, always trying to assess if anything has changed. Since we cannot see (the windows are still covered up), we listen with a third ear. There are no more sounds coming from the other room, and the silence is more unsettling than the noises had been.

Have they left for good? Will they destroy the house as soon as they withdraw? What will happen next? Nothing but silence. This is an oppressively silent night. Ominous and frightening. Minutes feel like hours. The tension is almost unbearable.

Magda decides to peek into the other room and silently, carefully, opens the door a crack. "There is no one there! All the Germans are gone!"

Sofia hears a noise coming from outside and we remain silent and still, not daring to move or look outside the window.

It is almost daylight when we are liberated!

CHAPTER 21

I Love the "Liberators"

Dawn, January 17, 1945

Without warning the door is kicked open, and six or seven men jump in, screaming and pointing their guns. They are surprised to see five women, two children, and a crippled old man.

"*Germancy,*" they shout, "*Gdie Germancy?*" (Where are the Germans?)

We stand up, our hands stretched high over our heads. Terrified, I yell back, "*U nas niet Germancov, Poshli!*" I did not realize I was shouting back in Russian.

Pan Professor shouts in Polish, "Welcome! Welcome! I welcome you, our liberators! The Red army is here! We are free! Thank you! Thank you!" He sits on the bed, his arms outstretched and welcoming.

Breaking the spell of this incredible moment is a man so tall he towers over the soldiers who lower their guns and step aside to let him pass. He enters the room and walks over to the bed. He takes off his hat and introduces himself. "I am General Markov, the commander."

Then he shakes hands with Pan Professor and tells him that he has decided to make his headquarters in this very house, which the Germans vacated just hours before.

General Markov is a very handsome man and I instantly fall in love with him. His chest is covered with medals and ribbons, so I know he is a hero! I am completely mesmerized by his dark blue eyes that seem to be smiling at me when I speak to him in Russian. He's taken with me also, and totally surprised.

"Where have you learned to speak Russian?" he asks as he strokes my hair. When his hands touch my head I remember my father.

After Kasia has looked him over, she decides to be polite and charming. Magda, as always, is very suspicious, Halinka is curious, and Gaby doesn't care. But I am elated. I know Russian soldiers, I've seen them before. For a while I follow the general wherever he goes.

In the meantime he orders the arrangements to remain the same. We are to live in the bedroom but of course are allowed to move freely about the house and grounds. All of us are so happy that first day, we don't know what to do with ourselves.

We hug and we kiss, my brother and I, over and over again. I sing and dance and run around in circles. Finally, Gaby reminds me that there is work to be done. The manure has accumulated for days and has to be shoveled out, the cows' udders are leaking, and the chickens have laid their eggs all over the barn. The sows are screaming with hunger and the horses also have to be fed. Back to work, back to life on the farm. No more Germans; now the Russians are here. Hallelujah!

Our courtyard once again is overrun with men and with machines. There are tanks and trucks and heavy guns with wheels, rocket launchers called Katiushas, the Red army's secret weapon. There are guards around the Katiushas; they are covered with tarpaulins and no one is supposed to go near them.

One can see that the Russians are well equipped for our Polish winter. Their uniforms are thick, yellow-green wool, their boots are called Valenky and are made of pressed animal hair that keeps their feet warm and dry. The hats are fur-lined and cover the ears.

Everything about this army is different from the one that left here just hours ago. There was something monstrous about the German soldier. He was mean and cold but always elegant. There is something primitive, almost barbaric about the Russian. His eyes are too intense. Sometimes smiling warm and friendly, sometimes lecherous and frightening—they drink too much, they sing too loud . . . and seem completely undisciplined.

They start in on the girls. A man grabs Sofia and tries to hold her and kiss her. General Markov advises us not to leave our room unless absolutely necessary. In essence, he implies all conquerors feel entitled to their booty. There is no booty here on this farm. Nothing left to take, only tender young girls. These men fought hard. For the past few weeks they haven't been with women; and now, drunk with joy over the last victorious battle, they want love. The message couldn't be clearer. The soldiers will do as they please and the officers, including the general, will close their eyes. Our sterling liberators are beginning to tarnish a little.

They are killing our chickens in a horrible way. They twist the necks with their bare hands, pull off the feathers, and throw the whole chicken into the giant kettle on wheels that is always cooking.

Two of our dogs have disappeared, and the barbarians have devoured my bees! I cannot believe my eyes when I see what these soldiers are doing. They have broken into the little house where we keep our beehives during winter. The bees have burrowed themselves into the wax honeycombs and lie dormant, sleeping through the winter. But the honeycombs have been filled with sugar beet syrup, and the Russians think it's honey. So they have taken out the trays and have eaten the sweet syrup, bees, wax, and all! All the hives are empty, the trays strewn all over, and my bees are gone, eaten up, consumed.

With the war here on our doorstep, we haven't been to church for weeks. Father Francishek came to visit us. He was making the rounds, visiting all the farms, warning women to stay out of sight as much as possible.

"There are rumors that some of these front line soldiers have just been released from prisons, and horror stories of their passage through Poland are starting to reach the church. Be careful of drunken soldiers."

But I know that Russians love children and I don't feel endangered. On the contrary; now I feel at times this war stuff is terribly exciting. No one else, only Gaby and I, are allowed to climb on a *Katiusha*. The soldiers touch and hug and kiss us with a great deal of warmth and affection, as if they were fulfilling a yearning they had for their own children.

General Markov has a daughter just about my age, and one day while we were sipping tea, he told me all about her. I reminded him of Tatiana. Then, in a truly affectionate moment, he gave me a present. It was a porcelain teacup of cobalt blue and gold, with two hand-painted cameo portraits, one of Lenin, the other of Stalin. It was magnificent, and I loved it. Everyone envied me, especially since I was the only one the general treats with such affection and generosity.

Magda, on the other hand, hates the general and me when she found out that he had decided to take her horse. At first she was so furious that I was willing to give her my cherished cup if only that would calm her anger. Finally her anger subsided, and she was beside herself with grief when she realized there was nothing she could do about it.

The general had a horse, a gray and white Percheron so enormous we nicknamed him "the monster." He was slow and thick-legged and very, very ugly.

Magda's horse, Kuba, was a young stallion, purebred and beautiful. Black as coal, he had four white socks and a white star right in the middle of his forehead. His coat was so shiny you could see yourself in it. And nobody could mount him, only Magda. She could ride him bareback, holding on to his mane. Everybody else cursed him, for he was temperamental even in the stable. He was stubborn and lazy and useless on the farm. Pan Professor had wanted to sell him or trade him, but Magda loved him and wouldn't hear of it. After all, he was her horse, and no one could do anything with him without her permission.

Whenever Magda was angry or sad or very upset about something, she would take her Kuba and gallop away. I think he must have been a racehorse because he ran so fast, and in minutes they would become a speck on the horizon. There was a special bond between the horse and Magda that was about to be broken.

General Markov had an easy time convincing Pan Professor that the exchange would be favorable to both parties. Of course he could simply have confiscated the horse; that was the way it was now. Those with authority took what they wanted. But he was a nice man, and I fantasized that maybe he was like us and that he felt something about Gaby and me.

Just before the Russians were to leave, the general came to say good-bye. It was then that he told me how glad he was that he had not bombarded our house, which he knew all along to be the German's makeshift headquarters.

"Had the Germans fired one shot from this house," he said, "I would have blown it off the face of the earth. You should be grateful to the German commander. He saved your lives. Either that, or someone was watching over you."

✦ ✦ ✦

It was mid-February by the time they were all gone. It took us weeks to clean up the house and grounds. Slowly we were becoming accustomed to the new expressions "during the war" and "after the occupation." We lived through the worst of times and now we are free. There were still soldiers around, and even explosions and deaths, but those were accidental. One of our neighbor's sons was blown up in the woods when he handled a grenade, like the one we found in our sauerkraut barrel.

As the snow melted and the mud started thawing, we found bullets imbedded in the ground where the Germans had dumped that whole truck of ammunition. This enormous deposit of bullets was regarded as a great treasure. Even though we knew how dangerous it could be to play with them, one bullet could be traded for just about anything, especially with the older boys, who knew what to do with them. I was the only girl member of this clandestine society, primarily because the bullets were on my property.

The arrangement was that everyone had a quota: five bullets was the absolute maximum. We would pry them out of the ground and then rendezvous in a clearing deep into the forest where there were many stumps of trees that we used to open the bullets. Slowly, the head of the bullet was pushed into the soft wood and then rocked back and forth until it was loose and could be dislodged from the shell. We then poured the powder onto a lid from a cooking utensil, and with a piece of string we made a fuse just long enough for someone who lit it to run far enough and be out of danger. Then we hid behind trees and waited for the powder to explode.

I hate to think of the punishment I would have received if anyone at home had gotten wind of what we were doing. Then one day we found out that the Russians were combing the woods looking for German ammunition. That put an end to our games, but by that time we were bored with it anyway.

The Germans left us their ammunition. The Russians left us their lice. For months we were infested and afraid we would get typhus. There were a few cases here and there in the neighboring villages.

Every day after dinner, Kasia spread paper on the table, and one after the other, she proceeded to delouse us. As she pulled the special comb through our hair, giant lice fell onto the paper, and we killed them with our thumbnails. That was our job, to kill the lice. Washing the hair was useless since there was no soap.

Magda and Halinka still had their long braids, and Kasia had just cut hers to look more fashionable. My hair was cut really short and Gaby's was barely visible. There was talk at one point about shaving off our hair completely, but Kasia was against it.

I remember at that time having my eyelashes trimmed by Halinka, who always contended that they were too long. "Lice could fall in and stay there," she said.

Eventually naphtha became available, the only thing that would kill the lice and the eggs. Kasia went to Wadowice, had to stand in line for hours, but came back with naphtha.

My head was doused with the foul-smelling liquid and wrapped. I wore this turban to bed every night until all the lice were gone.

CHAPTER 22

Now I Believe in Miracles

One day while working with him on the veranda, I noticed Pan Professor was staring at me. "Come here, Yanka, I want to look at you," he said. "You are growing like a weed."

The only mirror in the whole house was in the master bedroom. I didn't like going there to look at myself, but now I had a compulsive need to see. I felt awkward and a little ashamed. I was growing taller and felt my skinny body was beginning to change. I wanted to see myself in a mirror, to see what I really looked like. Could everyone else see what was happening to me?

Now that I had almost gotten over the frightening experience of the onset of my first period, I wanted to know if I also looked different.

When I started menstruating not much was explained to me, only that next month the same thing would happen again, and again every month from now on. Blood will come out of me and pain will cramp my abdomen. I was given strips of old white linen and told how to use them; they would be mine from now on. After my period ended, I was to wash them well and hang them on the line, where all the other women living in our house hung theirs. I was finally privy to the big secret from which until now I had been firmly excluded.

On this line hung flags of womanhood, markers of time.

It was all so sudden, these unexpected changes. No one had prepared me. There were no girls my age to learn from. Not yet eleven, I was too young to know. I knew nothing. But I was curious and kept asking Kasia, "What is a period, anyway?"

For days I asked and asked, and no one would explain. Finally I decided since the girls had dismissed me, I would ask Pan Professor.

Sunday afternoon Pani Ala and the girls went to visit Dr. Krawczyk. Pan Professor stayed at home and I was to serve him tea. When I came into the bedroom carrying the tray, the room was almost dark. With his hand he motioned me to the bed and asked me to sit down. He was waiting for me, and I, eager to ask questions, sat next to him. As soon as I sat down, I felt strangely ill at ease.

Without a word, he took my hand and put it to his groin. He held it down and I could feel the swelling. His breathing became faster and louder; he whispered something I could not understand and tried to push his other hand between my skinny thighs.

As I jumped off the bed, I tripped over his canes and sent them flying across the room. I knew something very wrong had just happened, but I did not want to leave the room. I don't know why. I stood in the far corner and cried. A terrible sadness came over me. I was alone again.

His voice was low and very gentle when he asked for his canes. "Will you please hand them to me? They are out of my reach."

Good! I thought. *If you can't reach the canes you can't reach me, so you can't touch me. I am safe.*

∗ ∗ ∗

In May, the war was over. Everyone rejoiced, but I started worrying again. I wasn't sure if I should bring it up. *What if I ask,* I thought, *and they tell us to leave?* Better wait for them to tell us. Was everything back to normal? I will wait for my uncle to come.

"As soon as the war is over," he had said, "I will come for you."

In church and at home, in hushed conversations, I found out about Auschwitz. The worst concentration camp was a few miles south of our farm. Finally we understood the stench the wind blew our way.

Dr. Krawczyk and his family suddenly moved to Krakow.

The Russian soldier who had been buried in the snow thawed, and we had to put him in the ground. His grave was right behind the fence. I worried about his ghost. I had nightmares about him, and about our future.

I dreamt about leaving and then having to come back. No one knew me; no one knew my name. And I could not remember it, either. I dreamt about a bear that forever pursued me; no matter where I hid, he would always find me. And when he was about to grab me, I'd wake up.

Sometimes I thrashed about the bed so much that Gaby would kick me, and I would be so relieved to be awakened from some terrible nightmare.

One hot Sunday morning in July, I awakened crying. I sat up in bed soaking wet, my eyes wide open, but I couldn't stop sobbing.

"What is the matter with you?" asked Halinka, who had come to wake us. "Come on, get up and get ready for church!"

"I dreamt about my parents!" I blurted. "I could see them so clearly. They were calling me, 'Yona . . . ! Yona . . . !' That is my real name! For the first time I remember it!

"They were on the road and I wanted to go to them, but I couldn't find the board in the fence that we lift to get out. I tried every board and they were all nailed down, but I knew that there was one that was loose, and I couldn't find it. I became frantic, knowing all along that this was just a dream, and that I couldn't let my parents out of my sight, or they would vanish. So I searched for the opening, crying with frustration, when you woke me up."

In church that morning I prayed for a miracle. Yes, a miracle. I wanted a resurrection. "God, maybe you can bring back my parents?"

Pani Ala told me that all the Jews were dead, but we were not to worry; we were not Jews anymore.

Was my Uncle Mooniu dead? Did she know for sure? She didn't know anything. He had stopped writing long ago, but she didn't know what had happened to him.

What will happen to us now that the war is over?

Now that the war *is* over, I think more often about going to school. Since I have never been in a classroom, I yearn for that unknown experience and hope they will send me to school someday, maybe this fall. I want to know what children learn when they go to school.

I am a country girl now, a shepherdess, a farmer. I know when to sow and plant and I know when to harvest.

I know by their scent the ripeness of fruit, into which pond the brook is flowing, and where the lily-of-the-valley grow. The forest is my playground. I know where to find wild strawberries, blueberries, and mushrooms.

Deep in the woods I know enchanted meadows. There I dance barefoot through invisible cobwebs, without music. I climb trees—the very tallest are my favorites; from the summit I can see to the end of the earth. I lie in tall grass and revel in the sun's rays that filter through the leaves.

I talk to animals and they understand me. I can read the sky and the stillness that precedes a storm. But I want to learn other things. For that I must go to school.

This is the time of year when we have electric storms. For the past few days the heat has been unbearable. The sun shines in the morning and then the sky gets overcast and heavy.

I am terrified of thunder and lightning, especially at night, but I love the torrential rains that follow. Everything feels better; after such a rain the air is light and cool and all the leaves are shiny.

Mushrooms grow as only mushrooms can after the rain. And when it's hot you can see them get bigger right under your nose.

Today's menu for lunch will be mushrooms cooked with cream over new potatoes, sprinkled with fresh dill, and plum soup. Mushrooms have been incredibly abundant this year (as if God had become aware of all the other shortages), and when they are in season we eat them almost every day.

I welcome the chore, since it takes me to the forest, where I can be alone. I feel restless today. I linger under the dense foliage where it's cool. The thought of digging for potatoes in the south field is not at all appealing—but I must do it and get it all to the kitchen on time. Without a scarf, which I hate to wear, the sun scorches my neck. Even through my blouse I feel it is burning. I should have done this first and then gone into the woods where it's shady and cool.

Since Sunday my mind has been elsewhere. It is the dream I cannot forget.

Ace, our old dog, is trotting alongside. I take him with me when I go to the fields because he loves to run through the furrows and brush against the plants. Too old to chase after field mice as he once used to do, he's content to follow me wherever I go. Ajax, our other dog, stays tied up in the courtyard. From the field I hear him barking. He sounds terribly agitated. Ace's ears are up and soon he's barking too.

"Stop it!" I command. But he doesn't obey me. "If you won't stop, go home! Go on! Your barking is driving me crazy. Go!" I scream at Ace, and point with my hand the way home.

At that moment, I notice Magda, who is trying to catch my attention. She calls, "Yanka, come on home." She's waving her arms, beckoning me to come.

"I haven't got enough potatoes."

"It doesn't matter, come!" she keeps insisting.

"Why? Why are the dogs barking?"

"We have visitors. Come on, hurry!"

"Visitors?" I wonder who they might be, since the dogs obviously don't know them. I walk slowly uphill. Filled with potatoes, the basket is heavy.

In the orchard behind the stables, Gaby is picking plums. He's way up high in the tree trying to pick the ripest fruit he can reach.

Two strange men are standing under the tree looking up, waiting for him to descend. As soon as he is within reach, they help him down. The older man looks foreign. He is holding Gaby by the shoulders while he's talking to him. My brother looks frightened. He wrestles himself free and is about to run away when he sees me approaching.

Pan Professor is talking to the two men and Pani Ala and Kasia—everyone is here. They are all waiting for me, I can tell, since they all look in my direction. Immediately I assume we have been denounced. These men are here to take us away. I know what I have to do.

I put down the basket and pull a thick stick from the woven fence. With it in hand, I walk slowly toward the group. They stop talking and everyone is looking at me.

My heart and mind are speeding. Think fast! Cause a distraction! I will strike them on their knees—that will create confusion long enough to grab Gaby and run for the woods—about a hundred meters between safety and us.

"Come here, Yanka, this is . . ." Pan Professor, pointing at the strangers, stops in midsentence.

The older man, who is peculiarly dressed in a red plaid hunting jacket and black boots, has turned toward me. We are facing each other, not knowing what to expect, like some kind of dualists, alert and silent. I'm ready.

I feel very strange, the few yards between us the depth of an ocean, the air heavy and dense. My heart keeps on racing, but I'm no longer afraid. I don't exactly know why.

I cannot move out from under his gaze. I stare back, fascinated by his glasses, which have only one transparent lens; the other one is opaque, sort of a milky white. I cannot disengage my eyes from his.

"Yanka, do you know this gentleman?" Pan Professor, the first one to speak again, asks me softly.

I don't. But I don't want to say so. For some reason I feel I should be brave and self-assured. "Well . . . I don't know exactly who he is, but I think I know him from before the war."

The stranger is visibly stunned by my reply. He gasps . . . in his eyes, disbelief. He opens his mouth as if to ask me a question . . . and suddenly I cannot breathe. I cannot move! Lightning has riveted me to the ground. Electricity has gone through my body. I want to scream but the scream dies and a wail comes out of my throat.

"Daddy, my daddy!"

THIS IS MY FATHER STANDING HERE BEFORE ME!!!

"Yonusiu, my child!" He calls me by my real name. His arms surround me and I know! I have no doubts! Everybody knows. It is my father. My father. My father.

The rest is like a dream. Everyone is crying, even Pan Professor. I cry also, and I laugh, I don't know what to do. I want to touch him but I don't know how. I am beside myself with joy, and terrified that something might happen and he will disappear again. I don't know what I'm feeling; everything is jumbled.

The clothes I am wearing are so old and tattered I am embarrassed when I realize what I must look like to my own, real father. I run to change into my one and only Sunday dress. When I come back, all spruced up with a bow in my hair, my status has changed dramatically. I am somebody's child!

It's finished. It's over—the fear, the doubt, all gone. We will pack our belongings and go home with my father. We have a name, we have a family. We are not lost or forgotten. What if he has no space for us? Gaby and I will sleep together. I must tell him. There will be no problems as far as we are concerned. We can sleep on the floor, on a mattress filled with straw. Anything will do, but he must take us with him.

"Where are we going to live when you take us home with you?"

"In Krakow, we are staying with friends for the moment, but soon we will have our own apartment."

"When should I be ready to go?"

"Soon, we should leave here before night falls. Where is Gaby? I haven't seen him since lunch."

At the mention of Gaby, Pan Professor clears his throat and with some embarrassment, says, "Apropos of Gaby, I don't know if I can let you take him."

"I don't understand, what do you mean?"

"Well, you see, Mauricy Spira, Gaby's father, made me responsible for these two children. There was never any mention of a Dr. Philip Kunstler. Of course, Yanka recognized you as her father, and since there is no doubt in her mind who you are, I will let her go with you, but I will wait for Spira to come and claim his son—who doesn't seem to know that you are his uncle. Why do you think Pan Spira never told me of your existence?"

"How can I answer for him? I don't really know why he didn't tell you. Maybe it complicated matters, since you told me yourself the children had papers as brother and sister. Maybe he thought we were dead, maybe he didn't get my letters. Who knows?"

I know! Now I must tell him of that day I remember so well, when Mooniu came home to tell me they were dead. "Uncle Mooniu received a telegram from Mr. Weiss from Sweden telling him you died on your way to America."

My father is flabbergasted! "I wonder who gave Mr. Weiss this information, but I understand now why Mooniu never mentioned our existence. He thought we were dead.

"In 1940, my wife and I were deported to Siberia as political prisoners and sent to a labor camp. I knew of the harsh conditions there from letters written by friends who had been caught and deported before me. When they came to take us that night, I made a split-second decision to leave my daughter with my sister, Regina. I knew she would take very good care of my child. Who could have known what was going to happen?

"When Germany attacked Russia in 1941, alliances changed. Poland became an ally of the Soviet Union. We were freed from the labor camps and relocated in the southern republic of Kazakhstan. We settled in Djambul, a large Moslem city, where we lived until the end of the war.

"In the meantime, I was chosen by the Polish government, which had formed in exile in London, to be their official representative. With this dubious diplomatic status, I became the protector of the Polish community of deportees, which comprised, among others, many intellectuals and professionals.

"There was enormous pressure from the Russians for us to become Soviet citizens—they wanted to keep us, and we wanted to go home. I knew that if we were to accept their offer, which they made very attractive, they would never let us leave. Each time the offer was made and each time it was refused, I went to prison, since I was the spokesman. Somehow I managed to survive it all. The will to live, to come back home and see my child, was greater than anything the Russians could do to me.

"As soon as Germany capitulated, my wife sold everything that was salable: clothing jewelry, everything we had. We bought identity papers and travel permits, which allowed us to leave—literally on the heels of the Red army. We arrived in Krakow a few days ago. That's when I started searching.

"It is really a miracle that I found out about you. If I hadn't run into Wladek, who had worked for Mooniu, I would probably never have found out where the children were. As he himself told me, 'Sent to the country a few years ago, but who knows what happened since then?'"

At that moment I realized why the other man also looked so familiar. Poor Wladek, the loyal employee my uncle sent to get me out of the ghetto in Tarnopol, and I didn't even recognize him either. He was working in the warehouse where we had been hiding before Professor M. brought us to live on the farm. He was the only one who knew about the connection between my uncle Mooniu and Professor M. That bit of information was the link that allowed my father to find us.

Why does it take so long for the sun to set today? I want it to go down faster toward the horizon. A mellow orange hue is finally flooding the garden. I must pack my belongings. There isn't much. My best clothes I outgrew long ago; the rest are faded and threadbare. Halinka's hand-me-down sandals have big holes in the soles. There is a pair of long stockings, a pair of white socks, and a few pretty round pebbles I found in the brook. Pressed flowers. And white lace gloves and the candle from my first communion.

I must pack the dress I'm wearing as it has great meaning to me. This white dress had also belonged to Halinka. I was lucky she outgrew it in time for me to wear it to my first communion. I waited for that dress for a very long time. When it became mine, I wore it to church on Sunday, for special occasions, receptions, and holidays. Today I wore it for my father. I must not forget my porcelain cup, my prayer book, and my rosary.

The prayer book is a jewel. I am the envy of the whole catechism class. Nobody has anything like this. It's a small book, very thick, made even thicker by all the cards of my favorite saints, which I have stuck between the beautifully decorated pages. On the cover, which is made of genuine mother-of-pearl, is a picture of the Madonna. It is carved into the shell and painted. The crown and the halo are encrusted with gold. It was given to me for my first communion. That's all there is.

Now I am packed and ready to go. I try to find Gaby. I suspect that he has been hidden; he could be anywhere. I don't want to leave without him, but I want to leave—to leave this farm. My home. The forest, the fields, the animals, everything I know, for an unknown place vaguely remembered.

Dusk has descended and we must be going.

The good-byes are painful. I cry; I can't hold back the tears. They cry. I want to leave as fast as I can. I want time to fly. And I want time to stand still. I want to be in limbo . . . I don't want to get to my new home too quickly. I'm very anxious about meeting my mother.

We hitch a ride on a military truck. My father speaks Russian with the soldiers; he tells them a story and they laugh. I put my head on his shoulder, ready to fall asleep. It was a long day, maybe the longest day of the year—certainly the longest day of my life.

He speaks to me gently and strokes my head to wake me. I am surprised to hear his voice. The truck has stopped; it is time to get off.

When I open my eyes, I see lights everywhere. Electric lights! In the streets, even in some shop windows. The brightly lit tramway rumbles by, making an infernal noise.

We are on the outskirts of Krakow where the city begins. Wladek says good-bye and we part at the train stop.

I am feeling strange, becoming frightened. I ask about my mother. I don't know what to expect. I don't remember her face; hard as I try I cannot conjure up her image.

As we climb the stairs, my father tells me that my mother is hard of hearing. At the top, a door opens. How, then, does she know that we have come? Even before we reach the landing, before we ring the bell?

She sees me. She gasps! Her hands fly to her face. She looks and looks at me, her mouth open. She stops breathing. She makes no attempt to touch me.

Should I go to her? I don't know what to do!

He pushes me forward into her embrace. She grabs and squeezes me into her soft, fleshy bosom. I smell her warmth and feel her softness through the thin cotton nightgown. It has been years since a woman held me. The last one was my Babcia, and that was so long ago.

AFTERWORD

The news my uncle Mooniu got from his friends in Sweden that my parents had perished on their way to America was obviously not true. As a matter of fact, they were the only ones who survived World War II on either side of my family.

Uncle Mooniu died in Auschwitz. He and Marta were on their way to Hungary, but their driver drove them to the Gestapo.

My father had to go to court to establish that he and my mother were Gaby's only living relatives. Then we went back to the farm and brought Gaby home.

Myself, Mother, Brother, Father (1945)
(from left to right)

CONCLUSION

It was only after my father died that I realized we had never talked about the war.

He didn't ask, and I didn't tell.

Now I wondered why?

I assume it was to protect me from remembering.

As I try to remember those years so long ago, I think my father wanted to make life as normal as possible for me, after he found me.

But how does one do that after such a long separation?

You behave as if you had never been apart. You take up where you left off.

My daddy knew it was my secret wish, my most fervent desire to be allowed to be myself again, to be able to live without fear or shame, to be like everybody else.

All of a sudden I felt free to reveal all that I had kept hidden.

All the things I never told my father.

My Father

Made in the USA
San Bernardino, CA
01 May 2014